me by my performance in those wins. If I got three hits and struck out the fourth time, the strikeout was the only thing Dad wanted to talk about. "What were you doing up there the fourth time?" he'd say. "You weren't even paying attention."

If I hadn't known it before, I knew it now: These weren't just games I was playing. They were proving grounds for the future, where excelling and succeeding would determine my worth.

Finding Faith

My quest to prove myself on the basketball court and baseball diamond irritated some people. When we'd win a championship and take the platform as a team to accept a trophy, I'm sure some teammates looked at me thinking, *Glad that's over!*

They might have been happy to learn that I was about to undergo a life-changing experience—the most crucial one of all.

It had started years earlier, when I'd spent so much time at church in Oklahoma City without knowing why. I'd sat in the pew for 15 years, never understanding what it meant to have a relationship with God.

Mom understood. But she needed help to get through to the rest of us.

She got it from an unexpected source—the New York Yankees.

When we'd lived in Houston, the Yankees had opened the Astrodome in an exhibition series. My dad, having retired from baseball nine years earlier, knew all the players.

So we'd gone into the locker room to meet the guys. I'd seen Mickey Mantle again, and watched him unbandage his leg. Whitey Ford was there, and Yogi Berra, too. And all these guys were drinking beer.

But star second baseman Bobby Richardson was drinking chocolate milk. I thought, *That's what I drink!*

Later I told Mom about it. She said, "Let's see if we can find a book about this guy."

It was her way of exposing me to real faith. I thought I was going to read about baseball and the Yankees in the book. Instead, Richardson talked a lot about Christ and his own commitment to the Lord. He wrote, "You can have a personal relationship with Christ." It was the first time I could remember hearing that—or at least the first time I paid attention.

Hmm, I thought. *Interesting.*

So Bobby Richardson influenced me—right before Don Reeverts did.

I met Don a few months after our family moved to Denver. I was a high school junior, missing my friends in Houston, lonely and scared in this unfamiliar city. I kept asking myself, *How can my parents do this to me?*

Then I met Don—a handsome former college basketball player from Tennessee. He was there at the right moment, with the right style. He was quiet, patient, but firm on one thing: *Let's talk about Jesus Christ.*

First Don dropped by during basketball practice. When we talked, it was mostly about sports. Finally, I asked, "What do you do, besides watch us practice and hang around?"

He said, "Well, I'm on staff with an organization called Young Life."

I said, "What is that? What does it mean?"

I didn't know that this Christian ministry's mission is to introduce teens to Jesus Christ and help them grow in their faith.

Instead of preaching, Don encouraged me to question him. And his answers were always good.

One day after school, we were sitting in a restaurant when I asked Don to explain to me what it meant to be a Christian. "I don't get it," I said. "I've always gone to church, but I've never heard this."

He said the same thing Bobby Richardson had said in his book: that I could have a personal relationship with God through Jesus by accepting Christ as my Lord and Savior.

Bringing out a Bible, Don showed me John 3:1-4:

Now there was a man of the Pharisees named Nicodemus, a member of the Jewish ruling council. He came to Jesus at night and said, "Rabbi, we know you are a teacher who has come from God. For no one could perform the miraculous signs you are doing if God were not with him."

In reply Jesus declared, "I tell you the truth, no one can see the kingdom of God unless he is born again."

"How can a man be born when he is old?" Nicodemus asked. "Surely he cannot enter a second time into his mother's womb to be born!"

Don explained how sin had created an unbridgeable gap between God and people, and that Christ's sacrifice on the Cross was the only way to bring them back together. Finally, I understood what it meant to ask Christ into my life to be my Savior and Lord—to become a Christian—and why it was such an important decision to make.

Don added that at some point every person must make the choice to either accept Christ or reject Him. I was ready to do just that.

"Why wouldn't *everyone* want in on that deal?" I asked.

"I don't know," Don said. "It's kind of simple, isn't it? But for now, why don't we just talk about *you*?"

"Well, I'm in. What do I do?"

He asked me to follow him in a short prayer. It included confessing my sins, requesting forgiveness, and asking that Jesus come into my heart and make me a Christian by my profession of faith in Him.

Just like that, it was done. I was born again.

Now I understood what my mother was talking about.

"You probably won't feel a lot different," Don said gently. "But you are."

I began to see life differently, and I was surprised to find that my new viewpoint threw a wet blanket on my desire to compete in athletics—at least for a little while.

That was definitely a change. The previous summer I'd been a counselor at a baseball camp in Chandler, Oklahoma. A dozen counselors and I, ages 15 and 16, had worked hard to build a beautiful locker room for ourselves. But when I struck out three times during a game, my rage flared out of control. I took a bat and in five minutes destroyed what had taken a week and a half to build.

A kid named Mike stood there, staring at me. "You really need Christ," he said.

Now I knew how right he was. There was no more bat-throwing, no more violent tantrums at the tail end of a strikeout or a lost contest. I thought, *These are games we're playing. In the eternal perspective of things, they probably don't matter quite as much as I used to think they did.*

The absolute, hard-line competing on everything subsided. It seemed I'd gained perspective when I received Christ, a more eternal worldview, a better balance.

At least for the foreseeable future.

Gari's Story

I grew up in a family I loved. We had dinner around the table almost every night, eating Mom's great meals. My siblings and I learned to camp, hunt birds, and fish. As a little girl I'd sit for hours in duck blinds with Dad, freezing in the early morning, having to be quiet as he sounded his duck calls. Like Bo, I loved sports. My dad and mom encouraged my interests in golf, tennis, and skiing, and these became areas of success for me.

As in Bo's family, performance expectations in my family

were high. One of the main principles in my house was, "If something is worth doing, it's worth doing in an excellent way."

The upside was that it helped us work hard to do our best and reach success. The downside was that it became a measuring stick. If you did well at something, you were just meeting expectations with little celebration. If you didn't, the criticism came because excellence was always the goal. That could sometimes leave us feeling conditionally loved, even though our parents never meant us to feel that way.

There was something else our families shared: the abuse of alcohol.

I grew up in the "cocktail hour" era of the 1950s and 1960s glamorized in movies at the time. My parents had their drinks before dinner so liquor was a daily part of my childhood. I didn't think this was strange because my friends' parents were doing the same.

When my parents weren't drinking, life was peaceful and fun. When they drank too much, my siblings and I didn't feel totally secure because with alcohol you never knew what you were going to get. I certainly didn't understand the negative emotional impact the abuse of alcohol had on me when I was a child. I wouldn't fully understand that until many years later.

But I left my childhood behind when I started college at the University of Colorado in Boulder. Music was a big part of my college life, and I sang in a trio called "Folks About Towne." Our first time to perform publicly was in front of a large group at a Young Life event. After the program we were packing up our gear when a man named Bob Straun asked if he could speak to me.

The first thing he asked was whether I knew Jesus Christ as my personal Savior and Lord. The baffled look on my face probably told him I had no idea what he was talking about.

After I made a feeble effort to defend my philosophy of life (a mixture of Buddhism, Hinduism, and ideas of Ralph Waldo Emerson), Bob explained that Jesus loved me and had a wonderful plan for me. At least I think that's what he said. When he was done speaking, all I really knew was that my carefully constructed worldview had gone up in smoke. Five years of putting it together, and in only five minutes the false had been upstaged by the true.

I still wasn't ready to take the leap of faith. But seven months later, after singing at Young Life events around the country, watching Young Life skits, and hearing dynamic speakers talk about the good news of Jesus Christ, I finally heard the message.

On a beautiful summer night at Silver Cliff Ranch near Buena Vista, Colorado, I knelt under an immense canopy of stars and asked Jesus Christ to come into my life as my Savior and Lord. I asked Him to forgive my sins.

Immediately an intense wave of peace filled me from head to toe. I felt profound relief that Jesus knew me—and that He had the answer to every deep question I could ever ask.

Excited about my new faith, I soon introduced Young Life to one of my sisters as well as my parents. Eventually they received Christ, too, as did my aunt, uncle, grandmother, brother, and youngest sister.

As the fall semester of college began and my trio kept on singing, knowing Jesus filled me with hope. The adventure of a lifetime was about to begin.

HITTING THE WALL

As HIGH SCHOOL ENDED, I found myself standing at a crossroads.

In the fourth round of the 1967 Major League Baseball draft, the Boston Red Sox made me an offer—with a generous signing bonus attached. The idea of playing pro baseball was tempting. But the University of Colorado at Boulder made me an offer I couldn't refuse—a full scholarship playing basketball and baseball.

Deciding pro baseball could wait, I went to CU as a marketing major—with a focus on athletics. For three years I started as shooting guard. In 1969 we won the Big Eight Conference Championship in basketball.

College gave me more than a degree and the chance to

win championships—it gave me a new name more accept-able to me than Dudley. A friend inspired by rock-and-roll guitarist Bo Diddley decided the world should call me Bo, and the nickname stuck.

A new name was nice, but marrying Miss Right was even better.

It was no surprise that I'd be drawn to Gari, a girl so attrac-tive, not to mention classy, sweet, kind, and much smarter than I was. But even I was surprised when, after just two weeks, I said to her on the telephone, "I'm falling in love with you."

And she said, "I'm falling in love with you, too."

We set our wedding day for the following spring—May 23, 1971. I saw no need to wait longer. That was partly because I was sure I'd be drafted by a major-league team. But it was mostly because I thought, *I'm not going anywhere without her.*

End of a Dream

Since the Boston Red Sox had made me an offer out of high school and I had done well through college, I figured it was a foregone conclusion that somebody would draft me now and offer me a fair signing bonus. But I ended up with much less than what the Red Sox had offered. Still, I was in the minor leagues playing for the St. Louis Cardinals.

I was impressed that even as minor leaguers, we were wear-ing uniforms with the famous logo worn by the Cardinals. Almost every day as I suited up I thought, *Stan Musial, Lou Brock, and Bob Gibson wore this same kind of uniform!* When

I put mine on, it reminded me how my dad had always taught me to respect the fact that athletic talent was a gift from God—and never to take it for granted.

In the summer of 1972 when Gari was pregnant with our first child, I was grinding through a 135-game schedule. At one point reality hit me—it could take me 10 years to make it to the major leagues, and even then, I'd probably be a fifth outfielder playing every now and then, waiting for the next 20-year-old kid to replace me. I thought, *I could do this for 10 years and get nowhere.*

My goal had been to be a major-league player like Dad. *But maybe that was just about my own ego*, I thought. *Do I want to spend the rest of my life being a professional baseball player, possibly at the expense of my family?*

The answer was no. So it was a blessing that the University of Colorado asked me to take the position of Director of Development for Athletics.

Soon I was trying to figure out my new career in fundraising. Running onto my new playing field, I braced myself for the next challenge—raising a family.

Family Man

When our daughter, Ashley, was born in 1972, life *really* changed. Unfortunately, my "skill package" didn't include much preparation for parenting, and it showed. As a provider, though, I wanted to shine. I hit the ground running as a fund-raiser, learning a lot and liking it. It meant being away from home almost every evening, but that didn't stop me. In a couple of years I switched to selling real estate, and the pace quickened further. My first year I was one of the top agents in Boulder. Eventually I worked two years without a day off, having 15 or more houses under contract at all times. There was always something to do with clients or prospects.

Our son, Andy, came along in 1974. His arrival brought more joy—and more work—for both Gari and me. But for every 10 hours I spent with the kids, she spent 100.

One day she looked wearily at me and said, "Bo, do what you think you have to do. I'll stay here and raise these kids."

I didn't hear what she was really saying: *You're missing our children's growing-up years.* I was too busy competing as a businessman the way I had in sports. It wasn't until my kids were about five and three that God got my attention.

To do it, He used a wise woman named Helen Dye. Helen was a strong Christian who was older than we were and Gari's best friend. She and her husband, Everett, were my dear friends as well.

Helen was also very direct. I needed direct.

And on that day at our home in Boulder, I got it.

Gari and I and Helen and Everett were there, having a casual conversation about the kids. Ashley and Andy were running around the house, a little out of control. Suddenly I heard Helen say something that made me sit up straight.

"You're the worst father I've ever seen," she told me.

Her tone wasn't condemning. It was more like, "By the

way, you're not doing very well with this, Bo. Everett and I didn't do this right either, and we missed a lot."

Despite the humility in her voice, my jaw clenched. I wanted to tell her to go jump in the lake, or worse. Finally I said slowly, "What do you mean by that?"

"You're so consumed by your real estate business that you don't know your kids or what they're doing," she answered.

It was a two-by-four between my eyes.

Helen's message—and God's—was clear. Gari was handling more than her fair share of parenting, and I wasn't stepping up.

Gari and I started praying and resetting priorities, especially mine. *I'm out of balance again*, I admitted. *I need to rethink this. How am I supposed to do better? Where am I messing up?*

Gari and I kept praying and talking. By the end of the process it was almost as if God had spoken audibly to me: *I have no greater gift for you in this life than your children.*

I almost missed this gift because I was doing in business what I've done my whole life: Go hard, prepare, work, and deliver.

Things didn't become perfect in our family, but there was visible improvement. My 150-miles-per-hour overdrive slowed to 100. I spent much more time with Gari and the kids.

I'd made a course correction—at least for the time being.

Doing Good

By 1980 we were living in Denver, and Gari and I were happy about our situation in life. We'd grown in our faith and parenting skills. Ashley and Andy were excelling in school, sports, and friendships. It was time to branch out, to do those big things that really counted.

We'd already started teaching Christian Marriage Encounter retreats. Now we joined Helen and Everett Dye and our new friends Bob and Allison Beltz to start a ministry helping other young businesspeople give top priority to Christ and their families.

One of our projects was organizing a weekly men's Bible study. Bob Beltz was such an inspiring teacher that we soon had about 200 guys attending.

One day Bob told me, "We should start a church."

Having no experience in founding a church, I trusted Bob and listened. He explained that with all the men we were reaching, we should invite their wives as well. If we were going to include wives, we might as well have their kids come along. And if the whole family was coming, why not meet Sunday mornings and call it a church?

I thought for a moment. "Are you going to be the pastor?"

Bob, like me, was driven and confident—but humble. "I'm more of a teacher," he said. "But I know just the right guy to be senior pastor."

He sent me to a church to hear Dr. Jim Dixon preach. I knew right away that Jim and Bob would be a dynamic combination. It would be like starting a baseball team with Joe DiMaggio and Mickey Mantle; it couldn't miss!

I was so enthused that I started talking to bankers right away about helping us buy a building. No way, they said.

They couldn't loan money to "a startup church with no members."

So within a month I personally contracted to buy a building. My optimism was so great that I didn't stop there. Within six months I had another, bigger facility under contract. I figured we'd outgrow the first building before we knew it.

It was time to start fund-raising. I threw myself into the task, expecting a great response. In the weeks to come I talked to 59 people about getting behind the new venture. All 59 people said no.

Their reasons varied. Some said I was "draining needed capital from the inner city of Denver." Others said I was "sowing discord among Christian brothers." Still others said, "The last thing this community needs is another church." Some seemed to think I would be "stealing" people from existing congregations, even though my hope was to grow the church a few families at a time, mostly with families who didn't know Christ. Many of my local heroes and mentors opposed me and the church idea, which hurt deeply.

Gari would say, "Don't listen to them. Keep doing what you're doing."

The Beltzes, the Dyes, and the Dixons would offer similar encouragement. After the president of Denver Seminary where I was taking classes encouraged me not to give up, I hit the fund-raising circuit again, thinking, *This can't last forever. I can't go zero for a hundred.*

Since I'd contracted to buy the building and property myself, I was anxious to deed them over to the church at our first membership class meeting. Some people couldn't get their heads around the fact that I owned it; they thought it was so unusual that there must have been something sinister about it.

Or maybe the opposition was to my style. I had an attitude that said, "If *you* don't get it, it's okay—because *we're* going for it."

My impatient demeanor wasn't good. As Gari said, "Slow down, let them catch up. Give people time."

After Cherry Hills Community Church launched on March 7, 1982, and 350 people showed up for the first service, others had a chance to see and hear what I'd been trying to describe about Jim and Bob's ability to teach and preach.

Gari and I, Jim and Barb Dixon, Bob and Allison Beltz, and Everett and Helen Dye were relieved and thankful when so many came that first Sunday, and also when the church kept growing—eventually becoming a full-fledged megachurch with thousands of members. It touched a lot of lives.

Working as a volunteer CEO of sorts for Cherry Hills Community Church was my primary work for the next several years. I still had real estate deals going, but my heart was in helping the church get started the right way. I probably averaged 20 hours a week on it for at least five years. It was the hardest thing I'd ever done—especially when I was convinced that success was all up to me. I kept thinking, *I've got hundreds of families here, depending on me to make sure this works.*

Meanwhile, I was trying to finish that slow-motion master's degree at Denver Seminary. I went to class during lunch breaks and at night. It ended up taking nine years.

Whether I was teaching marriage seminars or starting ministries, it seemed I was the one getting blessed—and stressed.

And the stress was showing. My temper was flaring again, even at church.

But instead of scaling my schedule back as I'd done in response to Helen Dye's warning, I kept taking on more and more. There were just too many worthy things to be done. They all seemed to depend on me. And I definitely depended on my own effort to make them work.

As the pace increased, I started taking less time to think through decisions. Back then I had the idea that being quick and decisive was best, the mark of success. At one point I actually had a secretary who came up with a code word she used as a signal to slow me down. "Breathe," she would say, and I'd get the message that my pace wasn't good for me or anyone else.

On December 4, 1984, in the midst of the chaos, a banker friend came into my office. It seemed two of our mutual friends were having a cash-flow problem in their business and needed a loan. Could I help by signing two promissory notes? One was for $110,000; the other for $90,000.

"Absolutely," I said, remembering how these men had helped Cherry Hills Community Church just 35 days before in getting a loan of its own. Each had signed a personal guarantee then for $310,000. I thought of them as solid citizens, as committed to the church as I was, and good friends.

Since they'd recently helped me and our church, I was glad I could return the favor. I was qualified for the loans, and trusted that my banker friend was acting in full compliance with the law. Signing seemed kind of noble—another chance to be the hero.

I picked up a pen and signed the notes. The banker didn't show me any loan applications to sign, but that didn't strike me as unusual. I assumed he needed to expedite paperwork because he, as a banker, was helping our friends with the company they owned.

The entire process took about 10 minutes.

Later I followed up by having our two mutual friends sign notes to me for the same amounts of money I'd borrowed—so that I'd have a proper record that I was lending them the money, they were repaying me, and I was repaying the bank.

It seemed pretty straightforward. I didn't think that much about the whole thing.

Not at the time, anyway.

Burnout

The chaos of my work life continued. I'd already gone to work part-time for my friend Philip Anschutz at the Anschutz Family Foundation. Phil and I had become friends after meeting in May 1982, just after the launch of Cherry Hills Community Church. Along with my friend Richard Beach, we'd soon cofounded a camp for inner-city kids called The Sky's the Limit.

In 1987 I got a call from Irv Brown, my friend and former college baseball coach, suggesting I start a live radio show interviewing Christian coaches and athletes, allowing them to share their faith in Christ. It sounded like a great idea, so I launched *The Heart of a Champion.* That was all in addition to my real estate work and the parade of parachurch organizations I was trying to stay in front of.

Somehow in the midst of all this, I helped found a ministry for homeless people in Denver that became Providence Network. It took an immense amount of energy and time to launch that project, but it benefited so many hurting people and blessed me to see it become reality.

Everything was moving too fast. Would life spin out of control?

On September 8, 1988, it did.

That was the day Gari had sinus surgery.

It seemed like a routine procedure, and apparently it solved her sinus problems. But from the minute she woke up after the operation, she knew something was wrong.

Dizziness. Confusion. So much weakness she often couldn't get out of bed. She kept saying, "My brain just doesn't feel right."

At first the doctors didn't take her seriously. When a few finally did, they couldn't figure out what the trouble was. Her body was failing her, and so was every remedy the experts tried.

When I left for work in the mornings, she'd be lying in bed with towels on her head. "They've damaged my brain," she'd say.

I wanted to fix it—or for one of the doctors to fix it. I wanted to do *something*.

The doctors were constantly experimenting with medications. They'd say, "You have to try this for six weeks until we can measure it and know whether it's helped."

It never seemed to.

Emotionally, I was worn out. I tried not to show what I was feeling, but it was eating me up inside.

It didn't help that the pressures at work seemed to multiply daily.

Some of the problems came from my work with the Anschutz Family Foundation. My job was to read, review, and make recommendations on hundreds of grant proposals a year. And "no" was the answer to 90 percent of them.

That didn't make people happy—especially me. It didn't allow me to be a good guy, much less a hero.

Sometimes a grant applicant would say, "I need an answer right now. I can't wait any longer for your organization to make a decision." And I'd have to say no rather firmly.

The pressure was no better at church.

I would sneak in late, sit in the back row, and then bolt as soon as the service ended—unless I wanted to play "Twenty Questions."

One person might say, "Hey, Bo! I need to raise some money, and I need your help!" I'd think, *How about "Hello, how you doing?" first?*

I began to tell myself, *If I come to church again, I'll come last and leave first.*

It seemed there were at least 4,000 strings tied to me—pulled by people who felt they had a right to ask me for something.

I couldn't handle all those strings anymore. Even my kids could tell. Ashley said I was ready to blow up.

Was I burned out? Oh, yeah.

Way burned out.

Gari and I were both exhausted, each for a different reason.

We were in no shape to handle what was about to come next.

Gari's Story

My courtship with Bo was a whirlwind—engaged at three weeks and married at seven months. He was funny, successful, kind, considerate, and into music like I was. He seemed to care about what I was thinking and feeling, and emotions hadn't been valued much in my house. He was a believer, and we were sure God had brought us together. When we married, we made specific commitments about creating a home filled with love, safety—and no alcohol.

But when Bo left baseball for fund-raising and real estate, working months at a time without a day off, I began to think, *This is getting to be a bit much.*

If I tried to tell him so, his comeback was, "Well, I have to get out there and make a living."

What I heard was, *Just pipe down. Your concerns are not important.*

I knew Bo was driven to succeed. Whenever his clients and friends needed anything, he had to be there—sometimes at our expense.

It was affecting our marriage. Bo was getting wound tighter and tighter, doing all this business and volunteer church work. He did listen to Helen Dye's warning about his parenting, and our family and marriage improved with a healthier balance.

We also learned great lessons from videotaped teachings of Kay Arthur, founder of Precept Ministries International. I felt compelled to share one particular lesson with Bo.

It was on Romans 5:3-5: "We also rejoice in our sufferings, because we know that suffering produces perseverance; perseverance, character; and character, hope. And hope does not disappoint us, because God has poured out his love into our hearts by the Holy Spirit, whom he has given us."

Kay drew two principles from this passage.

First, God is either in control or He's not. She believed God is sovereign, and God allows everything that comes into a believer's life for His perfect purpose. That made sense to me.

Second, when difficult circumstances come, we're to persevere and stay under the difficulty, not try to wiggle out. We learn from our suffering to understand the lessons God has for us.

In other words, Kay said, don't waste your suffering. Be wise and ask the Lord how He wants to refine you through this difficulty; you don't want to go through it again in a different way because you didn't learn the lesson the first time.

Kay taught that God is constantly purifying us as gold or silver is refined—building a fire under us, sending our impurities to the surface. He skims that off, turns up the heat, and repeats the process until He can see His character reflected in us. Whatever the test—stress, illness, heartache—He has our ultimate good in mind.

At the time, I had no idea why we needed to hear that—or why I needed to share it with Bo.

We would soon find out.

After we had moved to Denver, we were fortunate enough to minister to people in our local country club. It was during this period that Bo met with his banker friend and took out the loans. Something about the men Bo was helping concerned me.

"Bo," I told him, "you can share your faith with these men, but you don't have to do business with them."

He didn't do any business with them after that, though we stayed friends. Neither of us thought much about it—at the time.

Life continued to go well for us. One day in 1986 I stood in my kitchen, counting my blessings. Cherry Hills had become one of the fastest-growing churches in the nation. The Christian school affiliated with it, which I'd helped start, was taking off. I'd begun to do some speaking, had taught a Bible course for women, and was doing some organizational consulting with Mothers of Preschoolers—also known as MOPS.

So with everything on track, why had Bo and I needed to hear Kay Arthur talk about what to do during difficult times?

After my sinus surgery in 1988, we began to find out.

I woke up after the operation into a nightmare—it felt like an electrical current was constantly buzzing in my body.

Home from the hospital, I developed severe depression and anxiety. I barely slept and was overwhelmed with sorrow and tears. A fountain of grief would constantly well up inside of me.

I lost 25 pounds in just a few months—leaving me under 100 pounds at a height of five foot four. But I felt like I weighed a million pounds. There was pressure in my head, and waves of vertigo would overtake me. It was hard to go anywhere, to balance or walk a straight line. I couldn't shop for groceries, drive my kids to school and activities, or accompany Bo on outings. I wasn't able to take care of my family.

The doctors didn't know what to make of all this, and I saw many of them. There were brain scans and blood tests, all with normal results. Finally, one doctor told me I had a severe case of clinical depression caused by the surgery. "Well," I said, "I can get over depression. I'll do whatever it takes to get better."

It was a brave statement, and I meant it. But it still felt like the Lord had put the "real" me on the back shelf of a dark closet, and I was lost in there. I was so sick I didn't want to live—but I loved my family so much I didn't want to die.

That's when I remembered what we'd learned from Kay Arthur. God was in control. I had to trust the Lord that what He was allowing was somehow best for me. Because of His love and promises, I might be a woman who suffered—but not without hope.

While Bo and I didn't turn away from God because of my suffering, I had moments of distress, and even told the Lord that I would never treat one of *my* children the way He was treating me—since I knew He had the power to heal me. But

I also knew He had lessons for me to learn. I was definitely being refined, and I didn't want to waste the suffering—which seemed endless.

Then one day in November I sat in my chair, working on a piece of needlepoint to keep my brain occupied. I heard the Lord's voice telling me, *You are going to be fully well someday. But it is going to be a very, very, very, very long time before that happens.*

I held on to that promise, knowing it might not fully happen until I was in heaven.

In the meantime, I checked into the Minirth Meier Clinic in Texas and spent four weeks learning about clinical depression, and the fallout of a childhood of criticism and alcohol abuse.

I began to learn new, healthy ways to live my life. Through various therapies I came to understand the bondage of many of the unhealthy patterns of my childhood. Being able to address them was like being released from prison, freed to live life in a better way.

I knew this was why the Lord allowed this illness. He knew what it would take for me to demolish my crumbling childhood foundation and rebuild upon His.

It was actually a relief when the doctor told me that I had a sudden-onset brain illness caused by my surgery. I knew how sick I was, and it helped to hear someone validate the illness and explain that I wouldn't even begin to recover for another year because of the depth of my depression.

After a month at the clinic, it was also a relief to go home.

Bo worked hard to keep the daily routine going and to stay optimistic. And we both hoped our lives would return to normal any day.

But life was about to take a very different direction—whether we were ready or not.

CHAPTER 3

OUT OF THE BLUE

WHEN I SAT DOWN AT OUR BREAKFAST TABLE on the morning
of August 1, 1991, I was already tired.

Gari was feeling a little better—but it was still hard
for her to do much. I was trying to take up the slack with
parenting and household chores, which weren't exactly my
specialty.

I also took on two new responsibilities—a pair of part-
time jobs.

One was serving as volunteer chaplain for the Denver
Nuggets NBA basketball team. The Nuggets' assistant general manager, Todd Eley, had heard me preach a couple of
times and asked, "Would you come be chaplain of our team?"

Twice I'd said no because I was too busy. The third time Gari said, "What if God's calling you to do this?"

I'd forgotten to consider that possibility. After prayer and more thought, I said yes.

My other new role was as associate pastor at a new church I'd recently helped launch. It was a sister church to Cherry Hills.

Sighing, I picked up our copy of the *Denver Post* and pulled out the business section. An article caught my eye, and I started to read.

According to the story, a guy I'd known for about 10 years had just pled guilty to bank fraud. He and his family owned three banks in Colorado.

He was the same banker who'd come to visit me seven years earlier, seeking my help for two mutual acquaintances who'd aided our church in securing a loan. I'd signed two notes enabling them to get loans for their business.

This banker was well respected in the community, but the allegations against him looked pretty bad. As I read, I was stunned to see my own name, too—and a mention of the two loans I'd taken out at the banker's request seven years before.

Putting the paper down, I frowned. I'd repaid those loans—and the interest—long ago, and the whole thing was ancient history. But I thought, *I don't like my name in this article. I don't like the association here.* It just didn't feel right.

As soon as I could, I showed Gari the story. We both recalled how she'd encouraged me not to do business again with these men, and I hadn't. I was starting to wonder whether once may have been too often.

Instead of saying, "I told you so," Gari reassured me. "I know who you are. I know your integrity through and through. I know why you borrowed money to help your friends. They'd just helped you build a church. You're loyal."

I called a friend about the story. "I don't like what this says. Do you know of any attorneys who can advise me on how I should feel about this? Because I don't appreciate my name being in this article."

I was mostly irritated, not worried. *How do I hit this head-on?* I thought. *Do I need to hit it head-on? Do I even need to deal with it at all?*

After getting the name of a lawyer, I called him and said, "You may or may not know me . . ."

"Oh, I know you," he said. "I've heard you preach. I've been to your church."

I told him about the article and the investigation. "What should I do about this?" I asked.

And he said, "Well, let's just go down and talk with them and see what this is all about."

It sounded reasonable at the time.

Meeting the FBI

First I was advised to meet alone with Mike, an agent with the Federal Bureau of Investigation who was assigned to the banker's case. My attorney had confirmed that I was not a target of any investigation, and he thought it would be the right statement to make if I just sat down and talked with the guy.

When we met, I knew immediately it was a mistake to be talking to him.

It turned out the FBI wanted me to wear a "wire," a hidden microphone, so I could get the two friends I'd helped with the loans to incriminate themselves in a recorded conversation. The agent told me that my friends *were* targets in the investigation.

"No," I said. "I won't do that. Even though I don't know those guys as well as I did seven years ago, I don't think they're criminals. Besides, I'm the team chaplain for the Denver Nuggets and the associate pastor of a church; I'll tell you the truth, but I won't slant the truth to assist you in making a good story at the expense of anyone."

There was silence. Then the conversation turned into the most intimidating one I'd ever had.

The FBI agent looked me straight in the eye. "Well, then," he said, "we'll just fry your a—."

His choice of words surprised me. "Can you talk that way to people?" I asked.

"Yes, we can," he said, his voice icy. "We do, and we will follow through."

Suddenly I knew I had a problem.

The meeting had taken an awkward turn, but it wasn't over. We were soon joined by the Deputy U.S. Attorney for the District of Colorado. After we talked for nearly an hour, he said, "We'll be back in touch."

The FBI agent added, "And this is not going to go away."

I had no doubt about that.

After the meeting, my lawyer didn't seem too worried. He was surprised at the way the agent acted but appeared to think the whole thing was not going to be a problem. Apparently he assumed it was obvious that I was a good guy and had done good things, and that the threats weren't worth taking seriously.

I wasn't so sure.

At the very least, it was a bizarre situation. When I told Gari what happened, she stayed positive and refused to criticize me: "We'll get through this. I can't believe this is happening to you."

In fact, she didn't say a single negative word about me in the weeks that followed. And in spite of her continuing physical weakness, she didn't collapse. She even seemed to grow stronger. She was switching into ministry mode, management mode, mothering mode. She started ramping up, calling on her mind and body to do things they hadn't been able to do for months.

As for me, I tried to figure out what I'd done that was wrong or illegal—and what to do about it. I went over the events again and again in my mind.

I recalled the 10-minute meeting where I'd signed the promissory notes for the loans.

Were we all moving too fast? Probably.

Were we all too big for our britches? Probably.

Should we not have been doing it? I didn't know.

At the time I'd signed the notes, bankers were often seen as a pristine group—like teachers or doctors—who helped you toe the legal line, not cross it. I had no reason to think there was something wrong with my banker friend's request.

Had I felt pressured to help them? No. I was glad I could do it and had wished I could help them more.

Their request had pushed the right button: "We need a hero. Can you be that hero?" I'd been only too happy to oblige.

I could only guess why the federal government was going after people like my friends—and now me. Maybe it was because of the savings and loan scandal—commonly known as the S&L crisis—that had hit the country like an earthquake, starting in the mid-1980s. Nearly a third of U.S. savings and loan associations had failed or were about to, partly because of the schemes of unscrupulous bankers. A few of those bankers were said to have friends in high places. Taxpayers were angry about having to bail out the banks to the tune of more than $130 billion, and some heads had to roll.

Whatever the reason, the government's goal seemed clear: to punish somebody.

Good guy or not, I was now in the line of fire.

The Snowball

A month after our first meeting with the Deputy U.S. Attorney, my lawyer and I received another call.

"We would like Bo to plead guilty to signing a false loan application," the deputy said.

So this is their tactic, I thought. *I told them I wasn't putting a wire on, so now I'm a target because I won't pair up with them to get these guys to incriminate themselves.*

The government had obviously revised its strategy to this: "Let's get Mitchell on a felony of his own, so we can do what we want—which is use him as a witness for us against these other guys."

I told the deputy, "Sorry to upset your plans. But I never signed a loan application."

I reminded the government that in my brief meeting with the banker I'd signed two promissory notes. Leaving my office, the banker had told me no more paperwork was required for the loans to fund. Later I'd had our two mutual friends sign notes to me for the same amounts to show that I'd loaned them the money, they were repaying me, and I was repaying the bank.

There probably wouldn't have been a question now if I'd written on a loan application, "Intent of loan: to help friends with cash flow problems in their business."

But there *was* no loan application. Which meant I couldn't have signed one, false or otherwise.

The deputy still wanted a meeting, though. So I went downtown again.

I sat at a table across from the deputy, who had a sheet of paper lying in front of him. "Now," he said, "we've had our investigative team and handwriting analysts study this signature. And we've come to the conclusion that this is not actually your signature. Would you agree with that?"

When he turned the piece of paper toward me, I couldn't help laughing. It was a loan application, signed with huge, looping letters I'd never use.

"Boy," I said, "that probably *did* take an expert for you to figure out that's not my signature."

"Whose handwriting do you think that is?"

I guessed it was the banker's. "If he needed something for his files, he probably just signed it."

"Well, now," the deputy said, "that is the conclusion we've come to. Here's his writing, and when we compare the two . . ."

If I didn't roll my eyes, I should have.

I wasn't going to plead guilty to falsifying a loan application when it had never happened.

So I said, basically, "Can I go home now and go on with my life?"

And the government said, basically, "No, no, no, we'll keep looking. We'll find something else to charge you with, something that fits."

When I walked out of the federal courthouse a few minutes later, it was hard to believe the conversation had actually taken place. I thought, *This is like someone calling you from the Department of Motor Vehicles and saying, "Hey, we've been videotaping you for the last 20 years. We're gonna keep studying the tape because we bet you have some moving violations we can heavily fine you for."*

Was it supposed to work this way? Could they go on a shopping spree through my life, looking for something to accuse me of?

I was beginning to realize that "just having a talk to see what this is all about" hadn't been such a good idea. I was now on the government's hit list.

Maybe I shouldn't have been talking to anybody, ever. I was going to bat using a toothpick against Sandy Koufax, one of baseball's greatest pitchers. I didn't have a chance.

I also began to think, *I need to get out of this. I need a real attorney who understands this snowball that's rolling down the hill—a snowball we keep asking the Lord to stop, but it only seems to be getting larger, moving faster.*

It was clear to me that the attorney I was using was not up to the task. Unfortunately it was too late to change attorneys, and we were advised to stay the course.

Investigated

Over the next few months, my family and I felt terrorized by the FBI and the U.S. Attorney's office. They would select friends of ours, seemingly at random, and knock on their doors during the day. Then they'd put on their tough-guy faces, flash their badges, and say, "We're investigating Bo Mitchell. We would like to know what you can tell us about him."

After shaking off the shock, our friends would respond that they couldn't imagine I'd done anything wrong and then call me immediately.

"Hey, what's this about?" they'd ask me. "We told them you were a great guy and they're barking up the wrong tree."

It didn't matter whether the government gained any information this way. Its real mission seemed to be harassing our friends in order to pressure me.

Next the FBI called, wanting to drive me around Denver so I could point out "where these Bible study meetings took place, where you were supposedly studying the Bible but we think you were putting together your next scheme."

I did it, twice. I took them to Cherry Hills Country Club. They demanded to see the exact table where we'd sat and studied Scripture. Our group had called itself the Lunch Bunch, but it seemed to me that the FBI had labeled us as conspiring bandits.

One day the pugnacious agent I encountered in the first meeting was driving me around South Denver. As usual, traffic was heavy. Suddenly he decided he wanted to take photos of a place I was identifying.

He halted the car in the middle of the street and climbed out. I stayed in the car as drivers swerved to avoid us. When he started snapping photos, somebody honked at him.

Enraged, he turned toward the driver who'd dared to sound the horn. "Eat s— and die!" he screamed.

When he finished taking pictures and climbed back into the car, I was relieved that we hadn't been hit. More and more, the agent was reminding me of a bulldog—or a lunatic. Not like the Deputy U.S. Attorney, who seemed like a great guy. He was always professional, calm—even when his message was hard, heavy, and intimidating. He struck me as fair, sometimes even protective.

He seemed like a good person to have on your side, especially with someone like the FBI agent around.

Too bad he *wasn't* on my side.

The Charge

In late September or early October, I received the next call. The government thought it had finally found something to charge me with.

It was "straw borrowing."

I'd never heard of it. It almost sounded like the government hadn't, either—like they'd had to research it.

It turned out there was a statute saying that if you borrowed money from a bank for the benefit of a third party, knowing the third party couldn't borrow any more money from that bank, you were taking the position of a straw borrower. In other words, you were a middleman who put the bank in the precarious position of lending money to people who couldn't pay it back or were at the end of their borrowing limit.

When I read the statute, I could see it described what I'd done. I'd known my friends couldn't borrow any more money. But I'd known *I* could. So I had.

I hadn't known there was a problem with that. I'd thought I was being generous. I was qualified for the loans; and, after all, a banker was asking me to take them out. Not only was he a banker, but he was a well-respected member of the community. So why in the world would I think there was anything wrong with what I was doing?

I know now that I should have slowed down and filled out a loan application myself. I should have put it in writing, "This is what I'm doing." I'd never tried to hide it. But I certainly could have been much more thorough.

I told the Deputy U.S. Attorney, "There was no money lost here. This money was repaid to the banks in a timely manner. Even if I'm telling you, 'Yeah, that's what I did,' doesn't there have to be harm to someone? Doesn't there have to be intent on my part to have done something wrong?"

But the government's answer was essentially, "No, let's not get hung up on those words. You technically did something wrong, so let's all get comfortable with the fact that this is a real good felony fit for you." It sounded peculiar and unfair to me.

I could feel my options disappearing. *Should I keep fighting, or give up?*

I couldn't help wondering what might happen if I told the government, "No. You bring your case against me, and I will bring 4,000 character witnesses into the courtroom and a lifetime history of paying my bills, not walking on any loan, and certainly not trying to commit a crime. So let's tee it up!"

Judging from all that had happened so far, it was a game we'd probably lose.

From the time we'd received that first call from the FBI, Gari and I had been praying that God would stop this snowball and halt the whole process. We'd prayed that the truth would be made known, and that we could stop thinking about this and go on with our lives.

Apparently God had other plans.

Decision Time

Everything was happening so fast, and I had to choose whether to keep fighting. One of my cardinal rules was, "Don't make big decisions when you're in a down time." I knew most people didn't make good decisions then. This was a big dip, but I didn't have time to delay this choice.

I weighed my shrinking options. If I pled guilty and plea-bargained—signing my name and going on with my life—I'd stop the harassment of my family and friends. Would it be worth it to gain that relief? If I refused, would it mean preserving my reputation—or would I ultimately lose it anyway?

I decided to ask the advice of one more person who had experience with a situation like this.

After telling him what had happened, I asked, "What do you think I should do?"

"What do you feel like?" he asked.

"I feel like I'm being blackmailed by the government. And in fact there's so little here that I've ever done wrong that it almost feels like a phantom blackmail, because there's nothing there to blackmail me with. But they keep coming with this stuff."

His big belly laugh exploded over the phone. "That's what plea bargaining is," he said. "That's exactly what it is, and that's why it's unfair."

He paused, and his voice grew more serious. "I'm advising you to hope and pray you can find something technically that you did wrong so that you can sign your name and move on with your life. Because they have all the money and power and time. And they will do their best to just keep ruining your life."

There was an awkward silence as I thought, *This can't be right.*

But it was coming from a man I greatly respected. Finally I said, "That seems strange to me—that that's the best course of action." But I agreed to think about it.

When I hung up a few moments later, his message echoed in my ears: *They've got all the time. They've got all the money. They've got all the weapons. You've got nothing. Sign the document and go on with your life, and be finished with these people.*

The choice was clear.

I thought, *I could be a snitch—stretch the story, partner with the government—and live with that forever. Or I could just stand up and say, "This is what I did, or didn't do," and live with that forever.*

Even the possibility of going to prison felt better than living with the consequences of slanting the story to save my own skin.

My time was up.

I knew what I had to do.

Plea Bargain

In October 1991 my attorney and I met once more with the Deputy U.S. Attorney and the FBI agent. Another conference room at the federal courthouse, another confrontation.

I was presented with the plea-bargaining agreement. It contained one count, a felony: "inducing, counseling, and procuring" bank fraud. I wondered aloud how I could have done all that in a 10-minute meeting in which I'd simply fulfilled the request of the banker himself.

Again I was advised not to "get hung up on the specific words," but to just sign the document.

Things weren't moving quickly enough for the aggressive FBI agent. At one point he was so anxious for me to sign that he actually stood up from the table and took a step toward me as if planning to physically attack me.

"Sit down," the deputy told him. "This is Bo's life we're dealing with here. We don't need to rush him into this just so you can go have lunch."

I felt like a notch on the agent's gun belt. I thought, *Maybe there's some bonus provision in his contract that expires if we don't do this before noon today.*

We talked about probation, not a jail sentence. They kept telling me, "You're going to get probation, but the judge has the final say. And 99.9 percent of the time he listens to our recommendation." They said they couldn't put it in writing, because technically only the judge could make the final decision.

I thought of all the people who'd told me to sign so that I could go on with my life. I thought of my family. I remembered the advice I'd received from my friend and two law firms: Plead guilty with the recommendation of probation, walk into court, and hope that the judge is reasonable.

Finally I took a pen and signed.

I looked at the signature. This time there would be no doubt that it was mine.

I wished it weren't. Signing this statement felt like lying, the first time in this whole process that I felt I hadn't told the truth—at least not all of it.

It wasn't a complete explanation of what I'd done. In fact, it seemed like only a tiny portion. It left out that I was just trying to help my friends and that the bank president himself had asked me.

But there was no point in going over that again. This was my signature, all right, and that was all they wanted.

One Chance

Because of the plea bargain, there would be no trial—with or without a jury. No witnesses would be called. There would be a hearing, presided over by a judge who would pronounce sentence. Although the Deputy U.S. Attorney had repeatedly assured us that there was a 99 percent probability of probation, he made it clear that it wouldn't be "official" until the hearing took place.

As the November hearing date approached, there was one opportunity to influence the judge's sentencing decision. People who knew me could send the court pre-sentencing letters, which the judge could consider.

When I saw those letters, many of them moved me to tears. The psychiatrist who'd been helping Gari wrote that my wife would be "very adversely affected" if I were incarcerated, that I'd been her main support throughout her illness. He called us a family of "extremely law-abiding and moral people," and said this legal matter had already caused us severe pain.

Phil Anschutz called me an asset to his company. He also commended my work in helping to start programs such as the camp for inner-city children, and said he hoped I'd keep working for the Anschutz Family Foundation for many years.

Don Reeverts, the man who led me to Christ, recounted our long friendship. He vouched for my character and envisioned a productive future for me in ministry and as "a definite asset to our city."

Bill McCartney, head football coach at the University of Colorado and founder of Promise Keepers, wrote, "I would trust him with all my possessions."

My longtime friend Richard Beach of Doulos Ministries asked the court "to find mercy on Bo so that he could continue to be a productive member of society."

Inner-city pastor and social worker Luis Villarreal wrote, "In my experience, very few white businessmen like Bo Mitchell have ever had the slightest interest with what happens in the worst neighborhoods of our city. I found Bo Mitchell to be different. He was different because of his commitment to Jesus Christ. Without this kind of commitment, that is, the decision to follow a life example of Jesus Christ, Bo would never have invested in our work the way he did. . . . I strongly recommend that he not receive any sentence whatsoever. And if any sentence is given, nothing more than a very brief probationary period would be appropriate."

Jim Dixon, senior pastor at Cherry Hills Community Church, expressed his gratitude for my role in cofounding and serving that congregation, graciously describing me as one who had "a great love of God and a great love for people." He added, "My hope and prayer is that Bo might now receive the same mercy and compassion he has so willingly displayed toward others."

There was even a letter from former U.S. Senator Bill Armstrong. "I would like to express my hope that the Court will see fit to grant [Bo] probation in lieu of requiring that he serve time in prison," he wrote. He affirmed that my life "reflects exemplary character, dedication to the highest standards of ethics and conduct. Bo Mitchell's outstanding service and faith have been an inspiration to me and, I feel sure, to many, many others."

Each of those letters was precious to me. Probably the ones that touched me most deeply, though, were from members of my family. My wife's letter included this:

I am more proud of Dudley today than I have ever been, through watching him handle and almost be destroyed by the most devastating, humiliating, frightening, humbling, destructive situation of his entire life. But he is still trying to be God's man through it all, and for that I admire him and love him.

I set the last of the letters down, grateful for Gari and the other irreplaceable people who'd written them.

Now all we could do was wait as the hearing approached. It was all up to God—and the judge who would, in many ways, determine the course of the rest of my life.

Gari's Story

When Bo came home one day and told me about a phone call—and then a meeting—he'd had with the FBI, I said, "Well, you've never done anything wrong! This is just a joke." I wasn't worried about it. It wasn't like having a husband who'd done some shady things, making you think, *Well, you should be getting a call.* This was so foreign, so out of the blue, so strange.

We didn't know then that Bo was already in major trouble. One of his "friends" had been misleading investigators for over a year about Bo's involvement in the 1984 loans. Bo had invisible storm clouds swirling around his head, and they were becoming a hurricane.

To put it another way, instead of starting with a score of zero as we assumed, Bo was starting at a negative thousand. We didn't know we should be hiring an A-rated criminal attorney qualified in this kind of case. Frankly, we weren't sure we needed an attorney at all.

If we'd known, we would have found different representation. A criminal attorney told Bo later, "If I'd had your case,

I would have made one phone call to the FBI and this would have been over with."

We knew almost nothing of the legal system. We didn't know anyone who'd gone to prison, or even anyone who'd been in trouble with the law. We'd never even watched *Law & Order*, a TV show that depicted the criminal justice system.

So the justice system was a foreign country to us. We didn't know any of the rules, culture, or language, and didn't realize we needed to figure it out fast. We didn't know how dangerous our situation was.

As our challenges grew, Bo saw me growing stronger. That's because the Lord stepped in. It really was His supernatural power. I knew it at the time; I could feel it.

Much of that power came from our willingness to apply His truth to our lives and be secure in His sovereignty. It was that lesson we'd learned from Kay Arthur: God is in control and wants us to persevere and grow.

So with God's power, I rose to the challenge. *My job*, I thought, *is to be stable.* I wasn't operating on all cylinders, but what little energy I had went to my family.

Our face-off with the FBI and the U.S. Attorney's office continued to become more frightening. We tried to keep our growing anxiety from our kids—which seemed fairly easy since Ashley had started college in Kansas and Andy was focused on his junior year of high school.

One day, though, Ashley got hold of an article from Denver's *Westword* magazine. It was about how the government was going after all these people—including her father.

The news story just kept getting bigger. God was in control, but we felt out of control of everything, with no way to calm the hurricane that was blowing our lives apart.

Even though the media rushed to say negative things about Bo, it was easy for me not to lash out. I knew my husband hadn't done anything wrong. If he'd done something wrong, I would have said something. Rather, he was an innocent person who'd been caught up in a major legal event. The government's plan seemed to be, *If we get this guy who's a pillar of the community and has a sterling reputation, we're gonna scare everybody else.*

Bo was out there pedaling as fast as he could, trying to make this better.

He was so naive.

So was I. The two of us had always thought if you played straight and honestly with people, they would play straight and honestly with you.

As the sentencing hearing approached, we were about to find out how untrue that could be.

CHAPTER 4

JUDGMENT DAY

THE NIGHT BEFORE THE SENTENCING HEARING on November 25, 1991, I received a surprising phone call at home. The Deputy U.S. Attorney was on the line.

During the last few months he'd usually sounded official, professional, neutral. But this time his tone was apologetic. He said, in effect, "I'm sorry we got you into this."

I remembered how, soon after the investigation had started, I'd offered him a piece of friendly advice: "When you get to know me, you're going to think, *Why did we do this?*"

Now he seemed to be admitting, "You were right."

When I hung up, I felt a little vindicated—but not much.

Then a chill went through me. Did he know or suspect something he couldn't come right out and say? Something about tomorrow? Was he afraid that the judge wasn't going to agree to probation?

I tried not to think about it; the stress was already bad enough. Even so, I gathered a few necessities together to bring with me in the morning—just in case things went wrong and they hauled me to jail.

The next morning, just before we went to the courthouse, our family and a few longtime friends gathered in a conference room where I worked.

Many of us were already feeling broken, crushed. Even with the probability of probation, we were worn out from the legal battle. Despite years of ups and downs in the real estate business, I'd never been involved in a lawsuit; fighting a felony charge was out of my league.

We'd met here to pray. As we did so for the next half hour, I couldn't help sobbing.

My good friend Richard Beach did his best to lighten the mood. More than once in the last few weeks he'd joked, "Bo, if something bad happens and you have to go to prison, can I have that all-access pass the Denver Nuggets gave you so I can go in the arena and sit wherever I want to?"

Now, in that big conference room, he lifted his head and stared at my tear-stained face. "What about that pass?" he whispered.

Gari and the kids, meanwhile, tried to encourage me with

a "treasure box" they made. They placed messages and objects in it as expressions of love and support.

One was a card from Ashley that said in part:

I know this is probably one of the hardest days you've had to face in your life. I am confident that what happens is for the best—we all have to trust God. He knows your heart—just like we all do. Your faith throughout this long process has taught me more than you'll ever know. So, see—it's already done a ton of good!

You are the most loyal, loving man, and even if you were to be in jail forever, I'd still be totally proud to have you as my dad.

All too soon it was time to head for the nearby courthouse. Finally managing to compose myself, I looked at my family.

"This is harvesttime," I said. "Galatians teaches that whatever a man sows, that he will also reap. This is harvesttime for your father and for our family. Some of the harvest is already bad; we know that. I have to go through this legal process. But look for the good parts too. There will be good things to harvest here as well."

I hoped I was right.

The day before, a friend had called and told me, "God has revealed to me in prayer that when the judge opens his mouth tomorrow, you will hear amazing grace."

I hoped *he* was right too.

The Verdict

The hearing room at the Federal Courthouse held few surprises for anyone who'd watched a movie with a courtroom scene. The darkly paneled walls, the flags, the judge's bench, the witness stand—it all looked pretty much as expected.

I'd been here before, about three weeks earlier, to submit my "guilty" plea. This was the final hearing.

The small crowd rose as a black-robed figure entered. Chief U.S. Judge Edward W. Nottingham Jr. sat down behind his gavel. He was a dark-haired, distinguished-looking man in his mid-40s.

He was not smiling.

"Please be seated," he said. "Government's case number 91-CR-334, *United States of America v. Dudley W. 'Bo' Mitchell*."

I knew the purpose of the hearing—to bring finality to the plea-bargaining process, including sentencing. The cases and facts wouldn't be presented. The judge would preside, calling as needed on me, my lawyer, the prosecutors, and a representative of the Federal Deposit Insurance Corporation.

The judge asked several questions, mostly for clarification. He mentioned having received the pre-sentencing letter from Gari's psychiatrist just that day.

The prosecuting team made its recommendation of probation.

After about 25 minutes, the judge said, "All right. Anything else? Well, I will hear from the government if the government wishes to make any statements."

The Deputy U.S. Attorney rose to his feet. "Yes, Your Honor. I have a few comments I would like to make to the court."

The stenographer's hands flew over the keys to record his words:

This case has been very difficult for me. I have to state to the court, I have mixed emotions about it. Mr. Mitchell has been very forthright with us and very cooperative in our investigation. Based upon the information that we have available at this time, I can say to the court that Mr. Mitchell is the least culpable of any of the people in the scheme that's before this court. Not every person who's involved in this scheme has appeared before this court at this time. But I can tell the court, based on what we know at this time, that Mr. Mitchell's culpability is the least of any of them.

There is another aspect of this case that I want to bring to the court's attention. And that is I really, truly [believe] that Mr. Mitchell is remorseful. And he's got the ability, based on the information I've received, to advise people through his ministry about the fraud that was committed in this case. In structuring any punishment in this case, I know the court has done this in the past, and I would strongly urge the court to include in any sentence a provision that the defendant speak to the public about white-collar crime and how he got in the middle of this and his culpability.

I'd like to talk about that for just a moment. I read a number of letters on the defendant's behalf, and they indicate—and most of them indicate and Mr. Mitchell has indicated—that his behavior involving these "friends" was an aberration. Based upon what I have seen, I believe that's true. And there in this case is the tragedy. The defendant's reputation, except for this incident as I have seen it so far, has been very good—sterling, as a matter of fact. I believe that's the word that Mr. Mitchell's wife has used. I'm certain that he felt that in helping his friends by being a straw borrower, that that's all he was doing—that is, helping his friends. In a sense his friends really cashed in on his friendship. . . .

The letters given [to] this court that I have seen have been truly impressive. In all the years of prosecution that I have done, I have never seen letters that speak so highly of an individual and from so many quarters of the community. The defendant spent, obviously spent a lot of time in his life giving of his talents, his time, and that is giving to the community and not taking away. That's why I think this activity was an aberration. And that, your honor, as I said before, I think is the tragedy in this case.

The Deputy U.S. Attorney urged the court to take my cooperation into consideration. "Thank you," he concluded, and sat down.

For a few moments my gratitude for his words nearly overwhelmed my anxiety. I didn't applaud, but I could have.

I was glad he had tried to tell more of the whole story, the part the plea bargain hadn't mentioned. It seemed to me that, for all its talk about wanting "the whole truth," the judicial system hadn't been all that eager to hear it.

That had certainly been the case at the brief hearing three weeks earlier when I'd entered my "guilty" plea. In this very room the judge had looked at me and asked, "Has anyone promised you probation?"

"No," I'd said.

I'd wanted to say yes, but couldn't. They hadn't quite *promised*, even though they'd kept telling me the judge followed their recommendation 99.9 percent of the time.

I'd wanted to say, "But let me add to that, Judge, by saying they've all *but* promised me probation. They said they couldn't put it in writing. They said you had the final say, but that you'd go along with their recommendation."

Technically, my "No" had been a truthful reply. But it hadn't been the *full* answer.

If I'd said, "I've been promised probation," the judge probably would have just pounded his gavel and said, "This is not happening today. You all go back to work, and I'll see you in a month." And then we would have started the whole process again, with the same result.

Finally the moment that everyone was waiting for arrived. I was instructed to stand as the sentence was pronounced.

Once again the court stenographer's fingers flew as the judge spoke:

> This case is difficult. I don't agree with [the Deputy U.S. Attorney] concerning the tragedy of this sentencing. The tragedy of this sentencing and the tragedy of many sentencings it seems to me is that the sentence of the defendant [is] visited on other members of the family. And in this case I'm talking about Mrs. Mitchell, who evidently is in such [a] state . . . that her health may be adversely affected [if Mr. Mitchell is incarcerated]. And that, I think, is a true tragedy. Because other than marrying him, she didn't have much to do with this as far as I can tell. That situation concerning Mrs. Mitchell gives me much pause and causes me to favor some sort of light sentencing here.
>
> In addition, it appears to me, consistent with what the government has said, that it was not Mr. Mitchell who concocted this crime—that he came into the crime at the request of [the banker], who said he needed him to do something for two friends who had previously given a lot of money to his church, and Mr. Mitchell went along with that.

As he continued, the judge stated that he had concerns about the two loan transactions. There was confusion, he said, as to where the total of $200,000 had gone, and his comments caused me great frustration. He was essentially asking whether I had kept for my own use $35,000 for some reason. He wondered whether my friends had benefited from the full amount of $200,000.

I thought, *What difference does that make? If I had kept all of the $200,000 for my own use we wouldn't be here now discussing it.*

The confusion his comments caused set a negative tone throughout the courtroom.

The judge went on to say,

And nevertheless what comes through in all of this is that Mr. Mitchell was not the mastermind of this scheme. He was not the bank officer who owed a fiduciary duty. He acted at the urgings of others.

On the other hand, I am convinced that these so-called white-collar crimes can be deterred, and they will be deterred, if a message goes out that people who are caught participating in this kind of scheme face more than a slap on the wrist. They face more than probation. They face jail time. And that purpose of sentencing, the purpose of general deterrence—deterrence of others who are in Mr. Mitchell's position out there today—requires jail time in this case.

Jail time.

I swallowed, and the judge concluded:

> Accordingly, Mr. Mitchell, on your plea of guilty
> to the one count information charging you with
> aiding and abetting bank fraud, it is the judgment
> and sentence of the court that you be committed to
> the custody of the Attorney General of the United
> States, and by him imprisoned for a period of
> 11 months.
>
> And that, sir, is about the lightest sentence
> that I can give you consistent with the need
> for deterrence and consistent with factors that
> dictate the jail sentence.

When I heard that, my first thought was that the government
had broken its "unofficial" promise to us. If I'd ever heard
that even one day in prison was a real possibility, I'd have
fought for my freedom and most certainly won. How could
I have defrauded a bank when the president of the bank was
the one who'd asked me to borrow the money and assured
me that I qualified for the loans?

Imprisoned for a period of 11 months.

When I realized what the judge had said, the blood seemed
to drain from my head. Dizzy and unsteady, I asked whether I
could sit down. When permission was granted, I did.

Things quickly became chaotic. Ashley started crying hys-
terically. The Deputy U.S. Attorney stood up again, protesting.

"Your Honor," he said, "I'm not sure you heard me. I said prison time is not merited in this case. There's been no money lost. He's been honest with us. He's been helpful in this case."

The judge's frown deepened. "I heard it!" he snapped. "Now sit down!"

I thought, *Wow. Something's wrong with this judge.*

Finally I stood back up, still shaky.

I turned to my attorney, who seemed more in shock than I was. I reminded him that I'd heard mention of self-commitment—turning myself in at the prison later—rather than letting myself be handcuffed and taken away immediately, which is what they seemed ready to do.

My attorney made the request.

The judge was reluctant, but said, "Because of Mrs. Mitchell's illnesses, I'll allow him a month to get his affairs in order and report to prison on January 6."

The hearing was over. I turned to Gari and the kids. "You go up to [the Deputy U.S. Attorney] and give him a hug and tell him thanks," I said.

He'd done his best. He'd been civil and professional throughout the whole process. Not being able to deliver on his part of the bargain was likely tough for him.

I reminded my kids, "Your dad has subjected us to this. I'm the one who's put us in this position by my bad decisions seven years ago. So we're going to make the best of it. There are only two choices when bad things happen: You surrender or you rebel. Well, we're surrendering—to God. We're making this a God deal."

Despite the pain and anger they must have felt, they walked over and hugged the deputy.

Then, as I sat down again and tried to get my act together, I noticed Andy, my strapping teenager, wandering off by himself. He seemed to be heading for the back hallways of the courtroom. *Uh-oh. Was he looking for the judge's chambers? Did he want to confront him, maybe start a fight with him?*

Somebody reeled him back into the courtroom. If he was trying to defend me, I appreciated it. But I thought, *Hey, pal, don't make things any worse.*

Besides, Judge Nottingham must have had his reasons. Maybe he just assumed he was helping the world by sending me to prison.

But "general deterrence"? I guessed that meant he wanted to make an example of me. I wished he'd just sentenced me based on what I had done—not on the example I could be for others. That seemed odd and unfair to me.

I didn't know what he thought of the letters my family and friends had sent. I wasn't sure what he thought of the Deputy U.S. Attorney's defense of me, either.

But apparently it wasn't enough.

The Aftermath

When the hearing was over, we drove home and were greeted by relatives and a few visitors.

Most of us cried. All of us were in shock and couldn't believe what had happened.

I looked around at the familiar faces. *I have let everybody down*, I thought. *I'm not sure why this has happened, but I've disappointed everyone.*

My next thought, though, was more practical. *I have to start preparing for whatever this new life looks like.*

The next morning Ashley and I started calling the federal prison at nearby Camp Englewood and asking, "If you are supposed to self-commit at a future date, what are you allowed to bring?"

We ended up making at least five phone calls to the prison, independent of each other and spaced days apart. Each time we heard a different answer. One person said, "Nothing. Just show up." That seemed like terrible advice. What about clothes? Medicine?

The only consistent thing about the other replies was, "One Bible, one hardback book, and all the pornography you can pack."

I felt like saying, "I don't look at pornography, so I don't have any to bring in. But thanks for letting me know."

So, with less information than we would have liked, we started preparing to do what had been unthinkable just a few months before.

For me, that included resigning from several positions of responsibility. In fact, it pretty much required me to resign from my life.

I started with Cherry Hills Country Club. The morning after sentencing I wrote a letter of resignation, mostly to make things less awkward for my friends there. When an officer from the organization came over to see how I was doing, I gave him the note. As it turned out, the club eventually passed a new bylaw barring anyone convicted of a felony from being a member, so I would have been kicked out anyway.

Next I quit my position as associate pastor at Greenwood Community Church, which I'd helped found. I stood in front of the congregation and told them how sorry I was.

I resigned from the board of directors at Promise Keepers. Since I'd been involved in leading so many organizations and businesses and small groups, there were others, too.

Resigning was easier than I'd thought it would be. It didn't feel embarrassing; it felt biblical, sound, and fair to all those institutions. It was the correct thing to do as a Christian leader.

You've done this, Bo, I reminded myself. *You've created this—not them.* It was only right to let people off the hook of having to explain my story over and over.

What *was* embarrassing to me was the way some people acted toward me. They said, "Well, you *need* to resign, because we can't associate with you."

Wasn't that what I was doing? Did they need to be mean to me as I did so?

One pastor told me, "I am really tired of thinking about you, praying for you, and talking about your situation."

Well, okay, I thought. *How about if I just go away? It would make life easier on you.*

Still, Gari and I worried about how some of these resignations would affect us financially. I wondered how I would keep the household going. Because of some real estate deals that hadn't panned out, we were in debt—already tight month to month.

One of my employers basically said, "We're not paying you anymore; we need to distance ourselves from you." I was an embarrassment.

But not to Philip Anschutz.

I knew the Anschutz Family Foundation had reason to separate itself from me. That weighed heavily on my mind one day as my self-commitment loomed—and Phil called me into his office.

It was a humble office for a man with his accomplishments and assets—just Phil behind a desk, with a couple of chairs in front of the desk and a sofa to the side. He'd been in the same office as long as I'd known him, since 1982 when we'd met at church and become friends. After the sentencing hearing I felt I had disappointed him. I was embarrassed to be seen at his company, where I worked part-time. *I wonder what these people think of somebody who's this much of a bonehead*, I thought.

But as I sat down in front of Phil, his expression was kind, his voice soft—even sorrowful. He said, "We're with you. We're sorry this happened. We'll close the door to your office and pick up our dreams when you get back."

As I recall, he added, "I know you were just trying to do what you always do, which is help your friends."

It was humbling, and an amazing, unforgettable statement of friendship. With his high profile and involvement in a variety of companies, it would have been understandable if he'd distanced himself from me.

Instead he said, "We will send your checks to your wife."

I breathed a sigh of relief. Phil's generosity would allow me to go to prison with at least a little peace about how Gari was going to pay the bills.

Phil was a stark contrast to another group I was working with. They knew us well, but acted as if I were Al Capone. They seemed to say, "Boy, we need to pretend as fast as we can that we've never heard of Bo Mitchell."

Phil more than made up for that. It felt good to be understood and supported. It made me always want to repay him for that kindness.

Still, I felt the most appropriate thing to do in most of my other leadership roles was to step back. I was obeying Scripture; at the moment I wasn't qualified to be a leader.

I felt that way about going to prison, too. I wasn't going there to be a leader, either.

I was going in to shut up—so I could hear what lessons God wanted me to learn.

Whispers from God

So far we'd assumed that I'd be incarcerated at Englewood Federal Detention Center, about 30 minutes from our house. My family and friends would be able to visit. It wasn't probation, but it was something.

Then, at 8:10 the Monday morning after the sentencing, I answered my phone at the office. It was my introduction to how things really worked.

A brusque male voice at the other end of the line informed me that I'd been assigned to a prison in South Dakota.

I almost gasped. That was at least 500 miles away.

"I—I thought I'd be going to Englewood," I said.

The man scoffed. "You're just a number in the system," he said. "You don't get to choose where you go to prison." The conversation was over.

Numbly I hung up. *What should I do?* I thought. *Call home?* Gari would need to know.

But before I could call her, the phone rang again.

It was one of the last people on earth I expected to hear from: the attorney for the banker who'd asked me to do what the government saw as "straw borrowing."

"Have you been assigned?" he asked.

"Yeah," I said, "as a matter of fact, just five minutes ago."

"Well, we can get that changed in 24 hours," he replied. "Here's what you need to do." He proceeded to give me detailed directions about walking to a certain nearby building in Denver, going to a particular room down a specific hallway, and filling out a certain form.

"How do you know all this?" I asked.

He said, "I know more right now about how the federal system works than any other attorney in this city."

I was in no position to disagree. I'd heard he was a high-class lawyer. And I knew he'd done a good job for his client, my banker friend.

And he did it—he got me reassigned to Englewood. I saw it as a miracle.

But why did he do it? I wondered.

I took it as a major whisper from God—a reminder that He hadn't forgotten me.

Not long after that I received another surprising call.

This time it was the banker himself, the one who'd asked me to take out the loans. He was already in jail for his culpability and actions.

"You'll be okay," he said. "Just calling to tell you a couple of things."

He explained a part of the prison admission routine called the Cold Room.

"They'll just sit you in there and leave you alone," he said. "It's all part of the brainwashing process, or the process of acclimating you to the submissive life as an inmate."

It was a pretty awkward conversation.

I couldn't tell whether he was afraid of me, wanted to find out whether I was angry with him, or just trying to help. I guessed he was just trying to help.

I appreciated his warning. But I couldn't help thinking that he could have helped so much more just by being truthful about my loans and my conduct.

Impending Doom

The holidays were not exactly happy that year.

We visited my sister, Lana, for Christmas, but it was a somber time. Slowly I felt more and more broken. My spirit was being splintered under the weight of what I faced.

How do you prepare for something like this?

Since the sentencing, I'd tried to keep in mind what Gari and I had gleaned from Kay Arthur's teaching about being refined through trials. I was determined to keep my mouth shut in prison, to fall on my face before God, and find out what He wanted me to learn. Gari and I weren't joyfully saying, "Hey! Wonder what God's got for us!" But we were thinking with broken hearts, *There's got to be an end to this. God's in control, so let's see what He has.*

We prayed constantly for His protection, for any word of comfort He could give us, for assurance that He was in the midst of this, that we hadn't slipped through His fingertips, and that He had allowed this to happen for a greater purpose.

We prayed these things as a family, though it wasn't easy. Andy was angry. Ashley was in shock, often tearful.

Gari was strong, supportive, and kept a smile on—even though she must have felt like crying.

It was like enduring your worst nightmare, and then waking up feeling relieved, thinking, *Oh, I'm glad that was just a dream*—only to find that it wasn't.

As bad as events had been so far—reading reports about myself in the paper, feeling terrorized by the government, feeling misled about probation and the plea-bargaining process—they were just a warm-up. Now I was crossing from the judicial side to the Bureau of Prisons, with no idea how life-threatening that might be.

As people in the households around us strung Christmas lights and prepared for the holiday, a dark cloud seemed to hang over the home of my sister and brother-in-law. Lana and her husband, Charlie, did all they could to help. They were very giving, and it was good to be with them. But when some other extended family members talked to me, they seemed to be saying, *You were stupid. You never should have been trapped in the process. You never should have talked to the FBI. You should have had a better attorney. You've fallen through a trapdoor that you never should have been near.*

As far as I was concerned, that phase was over and didn't need to be rehashed. *We're going to make this a God deal,* I kept telling myself. *Whether other people understand it or not.*

The critics hurt a little, but what hurt most was a feeling of impending doom, of imminent separation from my family. *I'm getting ready to get on a spaceship to Mars and be dropped off on a foreign planet,* I thought, *among people I've never encountered in my life, doing things I never even dreamed I would be around.*

I started bracing myself, thinking, *I can't do this alone, but with God, with my family, maybe we can get through it. It does have a beginning and an ending.*

Despite everything, some family members were finding a silver lining on the dark cloud that hovered over us.

On Christmas Day Ashley gave me a card with this Bible verse: "Blessed is the man who makes the LORD his trust" (Psalm 40:4). Ashley had circled the verse and written a message of her own:

Lately I've been looking at you, just amazed at how blessed I am to have you as my dad. Your faith is

*unreal. I don't understand how you're staying so strong
and positive through this. But I'm proud of you! I'm
proud you're my dad. I could never have the courage
you have to stand up in a terribly hard time and be
God's man. I will miss you so much. My heart just hurts
that you have to go through this. You have always done
such good for others. This whole situation is unfair
and confusing. I know we'll all grow through it. And
hopefully a lot of good will one day result. I hope you
feel and understand my strong, unconditional love for
you. You are truly the best! I love you, Dad!*

When New Year's Eve and New Year's Day came, though, we
didn't really celebrate. No resolutions, no looking forward to
the happiness 1992 might bring. Our calendars were already
filled with sad and fearful expectations.

We bore down, getting ready to face what was coming.
Let's do these things while we can, I thought. *Because after this
day I won't sit at this desk again, I won't watch this TV again,
I won't take walks in this neighborhood again. The things I'm
doing right now I'm not going to be doing for a long time.*

There was a lot of hugging, a lot of prayer, a lot of clinging to each other. That part may have been hardest for Andy,
who'd been angry from the moment my sentence had been
pronounced. His perspective was, "Okay, it's nice that you
all have God. But I'm done with Him."

I could see why he felt that way. I prayed it would be
temporary.

All I knew was that some part of me had died at that hearing. The best I could hope for was that the dead part was the bad part—the one God wanted to remove.

A Sleepless Night

It was the night before prison—January 5, 1992.

Gari and I sat together at home. I was watching her write my name with a marking pen—like I was going to summer camp—on the backs of a couple of white T-shirts, a pair of sweat pants, and a couple of pairs of underwear. They were things that at least one person had told us I could bring into prison.

The phone rang. It was time for another unlikely call.

The man on the line was a friend of mine—Dr. Bill Bright, founder of Campus Crusade, now known as Cru.

"Bo," he began, "I heard you're in some kind of trouble, and I was calling to see whether I could help you at all."

"Well, that's interesting timing, Dr. Bright. Because I'm going into federal prison in the morning."

"Wow!" he said. "How did *that* happen?"

I told him about the whole thing.

Finally he said, "Let me pray for you right now," and he prayed over the phone.

Another whisper from God, I guessed.

We had a subdued family dinner, and now we were all just kind of huddled there at home, trying to get ready.

When bedtime arrived, I couldn't sleep. Instead of tossing

and turning, I went upstairs in the hope that Gari would doze a bit.

I felt awkward, lonely. *I need to start preparing for the reality of prison*, I thought.

Sitting in the half-light, I found a new fear beginning to grip me. *Okay, I'm going to federal prison for something that happened seven years ago, and no one lost any money. No one was even inconvenienced except me. If they sent me to prison for that, what's next? This has no ending to it.*

What if the judge or the prosecutors or an FBI agent decided I hadn't suffered enough? What if the government started looking for ways to charge me with something else? What if I broke some rule or got in a fight that wasn't even my fault, and my sentence was lengthened? What if another inmate killed me?

I don't want to tell my family this, I thought, *but I'm never coming home.*

Some might call it paranoia. But that thought started to haunt me, and kept haunting me.

I started mentally digging in, pulling away from life as I knew it. I might never know it again. My top priority now was survival. *I've got to figure out how I'm going to deal with whatever's thrown at me*, I thought.

Sometime that evening I found the journal I was planning to bring to prison. It was tiny, barely bigger than an index card, bound in fake burgundy leather and printed with fake gold ink:

The Christian Pocket Planner
1992
Denver Seminary

It was one of those freebies filled with little calendars and spaces to note appointments and prayer requests. It even had an introduction written by Paul Borden, Executive Vice President and Academic Dean. Its ending was ironic and prophetic:

> Denver Seminary can't give you time, but we can give you this planner to help you to use your time well. I hope you'll live every moment of this coming year to the hilt and live it in the will of God.

I decided to write my first entry, even though I wasn't in prison yet. There was barely room to write anything in it. I'd have to keep things brief and write really small.

As I'd found with the plea bargain and the hearing, there never seemed to be room to tell the whole story.

Mars Landing

The day before my self-commitment, I had called Phil Irwin and Dan Hendrick, two of my best friends from college. They still lived in Boulder. Both had been great football players at the University of Colorado when I was playing basketball and baseball there. Of all the things I'd taken with me from my time at CU, my friendship with Dan and Phil was the best and most meaningful.

"I don't know what tomorrow looks like," I said, "but would you come to our house in the morning and drive us to prison? Because I don't know what's going to happen to Gari and Ashley and Andy after I'm dropped off."

My friends agreed. Their role would be to give moral support to my wife and kids after I was delivered to the prison at 10:00 a.m.

The morning of January 6 was uneventful as the minutes ticked by. We prayed briefly as a family—mostly for safety and protection and that I would have wisdom in dealing with others. Fear of the unknown surrounded us like fog.

Nothing felt right. Everything felt final.

When Dan and Phil drove up, we all climbed into our silver Plymouth Voyager van and headed to the prison.

It was a quiet ride. Usually Dan and Phil and I could keep things stirred up pretty well with conversation, but everybody was overcome with sadness. It was like driving to my own funeral.

Later Dan described what happened next:

> The closer we came to the prison, the quieter and more uncomfortable we were as the realization hit: Bo would not be coming back with us.
>
> We arrived a few minutes ahead of Bo's check-in time. Good-byes were said, smiles exchanged, and tears fought back as he walked across the parking

lot into a fairly nondescript door and disappeared. We waited a couple of minutes, looking at the entry door, somehow half expecting to see Bo walk back out—with this whole scene just a bad dream or mistake that had been corrected.

But it wasn't a bad dream. As I walked across that parking lot, I thought, *This is like I'm walking onto Mars. Here's this door. I'm waving good-bye to them, and I'm in another world.*

And so I was.

Gari's Story

When the judge said "11 months," I couldn't believe it. My gaze shot to Bo. He turned chalk white—then bright red— then chalk white again. I thought he was going to have a heart attack.

That's when he could have been handcuffed and taken away, had the judge not approved self-committing. I credited God's mercy for that.

As soon as the judge pronounced the sentence, the courtroom went silent for me. Suddenly I heard a voice in my heart—or my head—that said, *This will be the salvation of your children.*

I thought, *Wow!* Then all the sound came back. I saw Ashley, who was so upset. I could see that Andy was angry and hurt.

This will be the salvation of your children. I didn't know what it meant. It seemed strange; after all, my kids were both Christians.

But I knew God knew. I guessed He gave me that promise to say, *Hang in there. Good will come out of this. There will be a reason.*

After the sentencing, three or four friends came up to me and said softly, "You know, this is going to be something great for your kids in the long run." I wasn't sure what that meant, either, but it seemed to confirm the message I'd already received.

In spite of his shock, Bo also made a point of reminding the three of us that this was a "God deal." Again, Kay Arthur's principles were center stage. This was yet another chance to apply what we'd learned from watching her videotape over and over:

1. Have an eternal perspective.
2. Remember that God is in sovereign control.
3. Remain under the suffering and don't waste it by not letting God perfect you.

We'd been prepared. God had us ready. He'd known this was coming even though we hadn't.

Was it really a God perspective for Ashley and Andy? Maybe not at that point. But they did recognize that we considered this a "God deal." For the time being, they were probably just following along. We couldn't ask for more.

After the hearing, about 20 people came to the house.

They'd kindly offered to go through this experience with us. Not surprisingly, it felt like a funeral reception.

This group agreed to read Oswald Chambers's classic devotional *My Utmost for His Highest* every day while Bo was in prison. Bo and I would read it too. And together, all of us would treat this as a God thing, believing He was in control.

During that gathering, the phone rang. It was someone who worked for a politically conservative organization in Washington, D.C. "Do you have any complaints you want to make against Judge Nottingham? We've been watching this case and watching him."

Bo had been sentenced only two hours before; we were still in shock. "Who are you?" I asked. I didn't know much about them, or how they'd become interested in our case.

All I knew was that I didn't want to pursue it. We were too scared. We didn't want to make things worse. So I said, "No comment."

Later that day our good friend Dr. James Dobson called.

"Oh, Gari, I heard about this, and I'm so mad about it," he said. "You've got to come on my radio show and we'll talk about it."

I was grateful that he cared so much about what was happening to us. But I said, "We've got to get through it first, Jim. Then maybe we can do a radio show."

"Okay," he said gently. "But as soon as you're through it, you've got to come. This is not right. It never should have happened."

"Well, it did," I said wearily.

It was tough on all of us, but in a way Andy may have been hardest hit.

He and Bo had always been extremely close; Bo was Andy's best friend. Now, when the four of us prayed together as a family, Andy said, "Lord, where were You? It felt like You put the devil in the judge's chair, and we asked for angels."

It was also hard on Andy when word got around about his father's fate.

There was an article in the *Denver Post*. The headline was something like "Ex-Athlete Arrested in Probe of Bank Failure." Technically, Bo did go through a process of being arrested after the sentencing, but we thought the way the paper chose to present it made it sound like he was facedown in the front yard with five police cars surrounding him.

That version of the story took on a life of its own. Andy's friends would come up to him and say, "Hey, Andy! I heard that your dad was arrested in the middle of the night, and he was handcuffed and dragged out of your house and taken to jail."

So two days before the sentencing Andy gathered his basketball team together to set the record straight. "Look, here's the deal," he told them. "This is what's happened to my dad. This is what's going on."

After he explained the situation, he said, "I don't really want to talk about it anymore."

I was so sick it was hard to celebrate Christmas, and looking forward to our future was like looking forward to surgery. We dreaded it. As Bo's self-commitment date approached, Ashley and I made lists of prison's pros and cons to help us deal with our fear of the unknown. These were a few of mine:

GOOD NEWS

1. When we see each other in prison we will be able to share what's going on in our lives because we will not have as much going on people-wise—and no distractions like TV for our conversation.
2. We will truly treasure the time we have now.
3. Compared to a lifetime of 70 years, this sentence is not a lot of time.

BAD NEWS

1. Missing Bo at night.
2. My best time of the day is when he gets home from work, and I will find it hard not to see him.
3. Having Bo in a place where he is in potential danger and cannot leave.
4. The uncertainty and anxiety of the future.

These were a few on Ashley's list:

GOOD NEWS

1. We'll all grow through this experience.
2. I will and have learned to appreciate Dad more.
3. Others will learn from it.

BAD NEWS

1. Miss having Dad at home.
2. Can't call anytime.
3. Worry about Mom's health and Dad's feelings.
4. Stress on the family.

But Ashley didn't stop there. She added, "Do not be anxious about anything, but in everything, by prayer and petition, with thanksgiving, present your requests to God. And the peace of God, which transcends all understanding, will guard your hearts and your minds in Christ Jesus" (Philippians 4:6-7).

Each of us, in his or her own way, clung to that promise as if it were our only hope.

Because it was.

CHAPTER 5

A DANGEROUS PLACE

THE WALL OF COLD, GRAY BARS slammed shut behind me as I stood in the prison "trap," waiting for whatever came next. My heart hammered as the steel-barred door in front of me began to roll aside. This time the tinny voice from the ceiling speaker said, "I've got one leaving the trap."

Forcing myself to step into Cellblock A, I thought, *Everything I was afraid of was pretty accurate.*

I seemed to be moving in slow motion. I felt the way I had when the judge pronounced my sentence—in shock. I couldn't hold a thought, much less a prayer. I tried to be on my toes, alert, on defense—but all I could manage was inching toward whatever might happen next.

The door slammed shut behind me. I stood alone.

But I wasn't—far from it. About 100 men were crammed in the cellblock—a space about 50 yards long. The two tiers of cells were unlocked because it was daytime; some inmates played Ping-Pong or cards in the open area in the middle. The racket was deafening as they yelled over each other.

But no one was there to show me what to do next—no guard, friendly or otherwise, saying, "Come fill out your registration form and check in." I just stood there with my trash bag containing five pairs of underwear, one Bible, one small radio with earphones, and a few other items.

The crowd in the distance looked mostly younger than I was. I couldn't tell whether they were checking me out or not. I didn't know it at the time, but my freshly washed white T-shirt made me stand out like a strobe light. Most of these guys had been arrested on the streets of Denver, handcuffed, and brought straight to this place. They'd had no time to gather a trash bag of clothes. They wore prison-issue shirts and pants and shoes either too small or too big. Nothing they wore fit as well as mine did.

Suddenly, though, all this was pointed out to me. Out of nowhere one of the biggest, meanest-looking guys I'd ever seen stepped right into my face.

"That's my T-shirt you're wearing!" he roared. "And I want it right now!"

I froze. Being six foot three, I could at least look the man in the eye. But I had no idea what to say.

Fortunately, God did.

I heard myself declare, "Well, I just got here, as you know. And this is *my* T-shirt. I know this because I watched my wife write my name on this shirt last night.

"My name is Bo," I said, "and Bo knows T-shirts!"

I was borrowing from Bo Jackson, the great two-sport athlete featured in a national advertising campaign called "Bo Knows!" that was popular at the moment.

Apparently the large, menacing man was a fan of it too. He broke into a smile. Then his smile turned to laughter. Finally, without another word, he walked away.

I knew my comeback had come from God, since my brain didn't seem to be working.

It took a while for my breathing to return to normal. When it did, two other inmates approached me. "You did a good thing there," one said. "If you'd given that guy your T-shirt, you'd have given him everything else you have too."

Whether the inmate intended it or not, I took that to mean I would have been assaulted sexually. I was thankful to God—and Julie in the Cold Room—for preparing me to sidestep this danger.

You've just passed the first test in Federal Prison 101, I told myself.

But a new wave of fear swept over me—followed by a wave of disgust over how pathetic my situation was. *The good thing I just did was keeping this weirdo from taking my T-shirt? Come on. How low can we sink here?*

When I was finally able to speak, I asked the two guys, "What am I supposed to do now?"

They pointed toward the far end of the cellblock. "That guy up in the guard station will tell you which cell you're in."

"Thanks," I said, and started walking.

I felt 100 pairs of eyes on me, sizing me up. *Who's the new guy? What's he all about?* If this wasn't another planet, it was close.

Welcome to your new home, Bo, I thought as I walked the gauntlet. *Get used to it.*

I avoided the stares. *You're probably never going home,* I reminded myself. *Accept the facts. Your old life is over, and the quicker you adjust to being inmate number 23386-013, the better things might go for you.*

After what seemed like hours, I reached the guard's office on the second tier, overlooking the whole cellblock—anxiously awaiting what would come next.

The painful journey was just beginning.

Home Sweet Home

Sitting at his desk, surrounded by stacks of papers, the officer gazed out a big glass window. He was businesslike, but sort of friendly. I didn't know whether he was making an exception in my case, but he seemed to know he didn't have to push me around.

"Follow me," he said. We walked halfway down the top tier of the cellblock, passing one empty cell after another, each pretty much like the one before—housing a bunk with crummy-looking army-green blankets and little else. Most inmates were down in the middle area.

The guard stopped and pointed. "You're in here," he said.

The door stood open. No one was there. The guard walked me a little farther down the hall where I got a blanket, a sheet, and a pillow, then he ushered me back.

A cloak of sadness, doubt, and shame settled over me. *I'm not sure I can do this. Wow. What a life I've carved out for myself here. I must really be a bonehead.*

When the guard left, I explored my new home. It didn't take long. Pacing it off, I discovered it was just six by nine feet—good news for a claustrophobic guy like me.

The bunk had a two-inch-thick mattress that looked and felt like it had been there for 40 years. There was one metal folding chair, a sink, and a toilet with no privacy. Two small steel lockers were stacked vertically.

The glass-block window in the back was three inches tall and about eight inches thick. I could barely make out the light that glinted from the large rolls of barbed wire surrounding the prison. The front door was solid steel with a small window about three inches high and six inches long— just enough for the guards to see inside during lockdowns.

I'm pretty sure this is not where I'm supposed to be. If this is a white-collar prison camp, I've missed it.

I was sure the judge hadn't done this intentionally. Others I'd talked to were sure he had—that it was all part of the drill to mess with me. But I thought, *He has no idea how bad this is.*

In the middle of that tiny cell, I sighed. *Either the judicial system has no idea what the Bureau of Prisons system is like, or the judge is just having a lot of fun somewhere thinking about me checking into this place.*

Even if Judge Nottingham wasn't aware of the conditions here, he knew what he was doing when he sentenced me to 11 months. If he'd given me 12 months, I could have petitioned to have the sentence reduced. But with less than a year, no petitioning was allowed.

I did hold on to one ray of hope, though. Julie in the Cold Room had explained that for every 30 days I served with "good time," I would get three days off the end of my sentence. And someday, when I was transferred to the minimum security camp next door, I'd get three days off for every 30 I spent there. "Subject to change," she added.

She'd handed me a document that stipulated my mandatory release date—September 14. That was the longest I could be incarcerated.

If I didn't mess up, on September 14, 1992, I'd be out of the system.

That was something to hold on to. *Okay, it's January now. Can I get to September?*

It motivated me—and probably many other inmates—to follow the rules. *Keep your mouth shut*, the system was saying. *Don't compound your problem by getting in trouble.*

Still, September seemed light-years away. *I'm never going home. Something's going to happen. Some other charge will be brought against me. They're still looking at my 20-year driving record, and they're gonna find another time that I sped or ran a stop sign or something. I'm in here forever.*

I tried counting my blessings. For instance, I wouldn't have to worry about probation when my sentence ended—assuming I lived that long. Most inmates had at least five years of probation, if not 10, during which they'd have to report all their earnings, all their travel. They'd be chained to the Bureau of Prisons the whole time. I had no probation.

Most had restitution to pay too. I had none, thanks to the judge.

But didn't the lack of probation or restitution prove I shouldn't be here at all?

I brushed that away, telling myself, *Okay. God's in control, and He put me here to learn something. I must really be hardheaded for Him to use federal prison as His classroom.*

So from day one, I began to wonder: *What is wrong with me?*

Finally I set my trash bag of belongings down with a clunk on the metal chair.

Almost immediately another inmate walked in and said, "Follow me."

I obeyed, though I wasn't sure it was a good idea.

Who is this guy? Where are we going? Am I breaking the rules by doing this?

I didn't want to do anything that might draw attention. Some people assumed otherwise, predicting, "You're going to be like Paul in prison and help so many people."

Not me. *I'm going to shut up, fall on my knees before God, and learn the lessons He has for me so that maybe I can have another chance at life.*

That vow flashed in my mind like a neon sign as this guy led me to a cell in the corner of the block.

There a man named Kenny told me that *he*, not the guards, actually ran the cellblock. He controlled what went on day-to-day. If I followed his instructions, I wouldn't have any problems.

Specifically, he informed me that he kept the schedule on the two pay phones inmates had access to. I was allowed one collect call each day, and 6:10 a.m. was the only time slot he had available. I could take it or leave it.

I took it. Listening intently, I was sure he could sense my fear. To impress me further, he added that he had $50 million waiting for him when he was released. He'd earned it dealing drugs.

Prison was just "a cost of doing business," he said. His five-year sentence wouldn't last as long as the $50 million would. So it didn't bother him all that much that he was here.

As he talked, I relaxed a little. I didn't know whether he was really in charge, but at least he was making more sense than most of what I'd encountered so far.

Kenny ended with this advice: "Put on the coat they gave you and walk around the yard for the hour you have to be outside today. I know you probably don't feel like it. But do it. It will help you get through today."

As I left, I thought, *It's scary to think the guards might not be running the place, but it's nice to think that somebody is.*

A Wonderful World

After only an hour behind bars, I experienced my first prison miracle. At least that's how I saw it.

I was barely settled in my cell when I heard my name being shouted.

I stepped out and looked down the cellblock where the guard was standing at the railing outside his office, bellowing, "Mitchell! You've got a phone call!"

What?

How was that possible? I didn't know much about prison yet but I knew it didn't involve incoming calls. It was hard enough to call *out*, as I'd just learned from Kenny.

Who could it be? I strode as quickly as I could to the guard station, picked up the receiver, and heard a familiar voice. Ginger had been a friend since college, now married to one of my best friends from high school, Roy Wilson. She was a successful businesswoman.

And a resourceful one. Ginger had tried to think of a way she could reach me. She knew one guard in the federal prison system, but had no idea where he worked. So she found his number.

It just happened that he worked at the Englewood Federal Detention Center.

It just happened that he'd been on duty when I'd walked into the cellblock.

She told him my name. "Yeah," the guard said. "He just got here. Hang on."

As usual, Ginger's voice was cheerful, strong, and steady.

She asked if I was okay, and said she and Roy were sorry I was there. "What can I do for you?"

It was so encouraging to hear her voice. When our conversation was over, I hated to put the phone down.

But that call was only half the miracle.

The guard turned to me. "While you're here," he said, "you might as well call your family and tell them they can visit tonight if they want to."

I couldn't believe it. I knew that when Gari and the kids dropped me off, they'd wondered what was going to happen to me. By now they probably were scared that I'd been beaten up—or worse.

So I picked up the phone again. Gari had just arrived home. Now I was able to tell her that I was okay and that she and Ashley and Andy could see me that very evening.

A coincidence? We didn't think so. We saw it as another one of those whispers from God.

A few hours later, the guard came to my cell. "Exercise," he said.

Remembering drug-dealer Kenny's advice, I pulled on my prison-issue coat and grabbed my little transistor radio from Radio Shack. About 20 other guys were headed outside, and I followed.

The frigid January-in-Colorado air hit me as we reached the prison yard. We had a tiny space—about 100 feet square—to just walk around in circles, over and over. Not what I'd call exercise, but at least we were outside.

Marching around and around with the others, I switched on the little radio. I set the earpieces in place and tuned to a local channel.

The first song hit me like a ton of bricks.

It was Louis Armstrong singing, "What a Wonderful World."

I see trees of green, red roses, too,
I see them bloom for me and you,
And I think to myself,
What a wonderful world . . .[1]

I tried to clown my way through it, thinking, *Wow, what a joke! I'm in prison, day one, in the yard walking in circles, alone and away from my family, and I'm hearing this song?*

But I couldn't laugh. All I could do was cry.

I knew the others noticed but I didn't care. My brokenness was sinking in, and I couldn't stop it.

As I marched, a question for God kept coming to me: *Are You sure You're in control?*

Along with that, a crazy-sounding list of rules echoed in my head: *Stay on the lookout, mind your own business, don't let anyone touch you . . . and oh, by the way—don't forget that it's a wonderful world!*

Well, not at the moment, it wasn't.

Maybe this, too, was a whisper from God. But it didn't feel like one.

And those wouldn't be the last tears I'd shed in prison.

A Perfect Evening

Dinner was at 4:15 p.m., served in a room that had all the charm of a Siberian laundromat, and the food was worse than the ambience. I could only guess the identity of the stuff slopped on my plate. Each inmate ate with a tiny plastic fork about three inches long—too small to serve as a weapon. I started to wonder whether I might starve here.

But I didn't stay focused on the food—not when I had my family's visit to look forward to.

I didn't know much about visitation, since nobody had explained it to Gari or me, except that visiting hours on Monday were 5:00 p.m. to 9:00 p.m.

Shortly after dinner, I got word that I had visitors. I wanted it to go well, but I found myself overwhelmed with where I was and what I was putting my family through. By the time I reached the visitation area, I was in tears again.

The room was small, with several tables. Gari, Ashley, and Andy sat at one. When they saw me and how hard I was crying, all of them burst into tears too.

Our reunion was awkward. We weren't allowed to touch without permission, much less hug. Everything was monitored closely.

At one point, when I'd composed myself enough, I decided to try the vending machine in the little room.

A guard eyed me as I walked past his desk.

Out of habit, I asked, "Would you like a soda?"

The guard motioned me over. "It's not a good thing for

you to ask me if I want a soda," he said quietly. "Just go get yours. But thanks."

I winced, embarrassed. *I guess that does look like sucking up to the guards.* Guards were people, too, but it was clear there would be no friendly give-and-take with them.

It was a short visit, but it was better than nothing.

After an equally awkward good-bye, my family was gone.

I followed a guard out of the room and into another.

Where I was strip-searched.

They had to make sure no one had passed me any contraband—a weapon, a file, some drugs.

It was the perfect end to a perfect evening.

Lights Out

When I returned to my cell, I had a roommate.

I said hello. He said nothing.

In fact, he would never say a word to me—or to anyone else. I had to guess which bunk was his, and which locker.

I didn't know what his name was or what he was in for. I thought he might be one of the drug guys, like so many seemed to be.

All I knew was that he was about five foot ten and around 170 pounds. That wasn't much to go on.

Maybe he was a murderer. Maybe he would try to kill me in my sleep. Or was he a sex offender? Would he try to assault me in the middle of the night?

Eventually I learned the truth from another inmate. Sam

was in prison for attempted murder. He'd attacked his wife and children, almost killing them. He was awaiting reassignment to a "deeper" part of the prison system.

If I'd known that, I'd have been even more nervous.

It was going to be a long night. I hadn't slept the previous night, and I probably wouldn't get any rest now, either.

When "Lights Out" was announced at 10:00 p.m. and the doors were locked, I discovered my cell's location was a blessing. There was just enough light from the center of the cellblock that I could stand by the door and read my Oswald Chambers devotional book for at least an hour, trying to relax myself enough to crawl to my top bunk and fall asleep.

The sleep part didn't apply tonight, though. Besides the round-the-clock yelling of inmates, I was on high alert, not knowing whether my silent roommate might have plans for me. When I finally lay on that lousy mattress, I couldn't doze. Instead, I started thinking again.

I considered how I might defend myself. *This must be what it means to be institutionalized*, I thought. *If this guy touches me, I'll kill him.*

I couldn't believe I was thinking that way. *I guess I'm already reconciled to never going home*, I told myself. Yet I also kept reminding myself that God was in control, and that I must really have screwed up for this to be part of His perfect plan for my life.

How could I believe God was in control—and fear my roommate so much that I was ready to kill him?

Not all my thoughts made a lot of sense, but one thing seemed clear: *One night here is enough for me to learn my lesson, if that's what Judge Nottingham had in mind.*

But my mandatory release date was definitely not tomorrow.

Sometime that night I found my little burgundy fake-leather journal. I scribbled in tiny letters:

JANUARY 6: *I cry at the thought of my family . . . NO sleep at all. Very noisy. Guys screaming out like in a hospital. Feeling awful! Scared, apprehensive, ashamed, out of place.*

That pretty well summed it up. Putting down the pen, I stared into the darkness.

Gari's Story

My heart broke on that cold, dreary morning in January as my husband stepped out of the car, kissed me good-bye, and walked through the door of the prison.

I couldn't even visualize the place inside. I had the strange feeling that Bo was Alice in Wonderland and he'd just gone down the rabbit hole into who-knows-what. I had to put my faith in God and trust He was protecting Bo.

When Ashley, Andy, Phil, Dan, and I returned home, I thought of what our family had been doing there just a few hours earlier—eating breakfast and praying. Now Bo wasn't there. It felt so strange. We really didn't know what to do next.

We'd been told we wouldn't hear from Bo for a few days until he had permission to make phone calls or see him for at least a week. That was a painful prospect. For more than 21 years, we'd told each other, "I love you" almost every day. Even when we were apart, almost always we would connect by phone and say those words. And now—nothing.

I couldn't know what he was experiencing, who he was meeting, what was happening to him. *This must be how wives feel when their husbands go off to war*, I thought. All I could do was pray.

The kids and I scattered and the house was so quiet. We seemed to be waiting for something but didn't know what it was. I was frozen in disbelief that this had happened to our family—and especially to Bo.

My swirling thoughts and feelings were suddenly interrupted by the telephone. *Probably a friend checking on us*, I thought.

But when I answered the call an operator said, "Will you accept a collect call from Bo Mitchell?"

The next thing I heard was Bo's voice. He was okay—and we had permission to visit him that night!

I was astonished. He tried to explain what had happened, but I couldn't take it all in. When I hung up, I yelled for the kids and told them the news. Our joy lit up the house.

Driving up to the prison that evening, we didn't know what to expect. Confused about where to go, we kept circling in the dark until we figured it out.

We were nervous as we walked through the door and

checked in at a window. An officer told us to put our purses and coats in the bins behind us, and step through the door into a small hallway with a closed door at the other end. It was like a trap.

The door behind us clicked shut; a moment later the door in front of us clicked open. We walked into an area that looked much like a small high school lunchroom.

Finding a table with four chairs, we sat down. The officer called on a phone to say Bo had visitors. We waited several minutes. I could see the tension on Ashley's and Andy's faces.

And then, all at once, there was Bo, entering through another door.

But he looked so different. He was in prison clothes that didn't fit too well, but that wasn't the worst of it. His face was red, and he was crying and clearly upset.

This made us all start crying too.

He sat down at our table. We stared at each other with stunned disbelief.

I wanted to reach across the table to touch him, but it wasn't permitted. We were told there was to be no contact, and the guards were watching everyone in the room intently. It was scary and strange and sad.

Bo stopped crying long enough to tell us why we were able to see him that night—and that we could visit every night as long as he was there! Amazed, we realized the Lord had made this happen. He was already answering our prayers. I was so grateful that we could see Bo; I could tell he needed us desperately.

We hadn't been there long when a guard said it was time for Bo to go. As we stood up, I asked the guard. "Can I give him a hug and a kiss?"

"Yeah," he answered. "Very brief."

The officer watched carefully. It wasn't much of a hug, but it would have to do. We all said our good-byes.

I hated watching Bo walk back through the door. But I had to trust the Lord to keep him safe in this dangerous place.

As we drove out of the parking lot, we were all so disoriented—and crying so hard—that I took a wrong turn. A guard patrolling the grounds drove up next to us, saying we were going the wrong way. Finally we found the right road.

Driving home, I recalled how hard Bo had cried—and now we were all doing the same. I thought, *Someone in this group has to quit crying. And that person will be me.* I vowed that the rest of the time Bo was in prison I wouldn't cry unless I was by myself.

There were times Bo and I did shed tears together in the months ahead as we went through this sad and difficult time, but I was never again undone emotionally as I was that first night.

By the time we made it home, I was so full of pain and stress I thought I would explode. I was beginning to see that dealing with Bo's imprisonment would be unlike anything I'd ever done. I felt I'd been cast off a cliff; I was falling and didn't know whether anyone or anything would catch me. Nothing I knew seemed to apply here.

Even though it was icy, dark, and 10 degrees, I had to get out of the house. So I took our two Japanese Chin dogs for a walk.

I passed a home still displaying Christmas lights and decorations. On the very top of the roof sat a Star of David. It had always comforted me when I stopped to look at it. But that night, as I looked at that star, my feelings were much more complicated. I believed God was in control of everything, but I needed His right-here, right-now help.

I shook my fist at Him, telling Him, *You're in control, and You've allowed this to happen. Now You've got to send me something to get me through this night.* It was more a desperate plea than an angry request.

Somehow I had to be the leader of our household. I needed supernatural strength because I still wasn't well. I needed relief from the overwhelming stress and fear. I had to be strong for Bo and make our children's lives as normal as they could be in this abnormal time.

I needed a promise that things would be okay.

Back at the house, I started reading Psalm 66, looking desperately for comfort, help, and hope. Before I knew it I was reading verses 10-12:

> For you, O God, tested us;
>   you refined us like silver.
> You brought us into prison
>   and laid burdens on our backs.

You let men ride over our heads;
　　we went through fire and water,
　　but you brought us to a place of abundance.

The words were like burning flames on the page. These verses described exactly how I—how we—were feeling.

We were being tested, refined, brought into prison—but the Lord knew all about it. We had the hope of being brought to a place of abundance someday.

In the margin of my Bible I wrote, *These are the first words of blessing from God, the first night Bo was in prison.*

Like Bo, I believed we were in this mess for a reason. We were being sifted—an idea we'd learned from the Bible's account of how Satan asked God for permission to sift Peter in Luke 22:31. We were all scared to death, not knowing what to expect. But we trusted God would use this to refine and purify us.

I was able to sleep peacefully. God had spoken to me and it was enough—at least for that day.

CHAPTER 6

BEHIND BARS

It had been a long night. Most of the time I stood by the cell door and read Oswald Chambers just to get through. Finally I gave up on sleep and started my first full day in prison at 6:00 a.m.

I got in line for breakfast, not expecting much after last night's dining experience.

I got more than I bargained for.

Picking up a tray, I stood in line next to a short, overweight guy with a mustache and what looked like a permanent scowl. Another inmate on the kitchen side scooped nondescript food onto our plates as we moved along.

Suddenly the guy next to me picked up his tray and flung

it in the face of the inmate who'd just filled it. Food flew everywhere. The plate clattered to the floor.

Startled, I stepped back. The rage on the thrower's face said he was mad at everybody, everything. Mad at the world.

I knew he hadn't done himself any favors with his impulsive act. The guards probably would be here any second. Breaking the rules was futile at best, self-destructive at worst.

But that wasn't uppermost in my mind as I moved farther down the line. I mostly feared the unpredictability. *Anything can happen at any time*, I reminded myself, *and probably will.*

This really *was* a dangerous place. *Watch out*, I told myself.

God's Hand

Later that morning I managed to call Gari. There were plenty of things we could have talked about, including the tray-throwing in the mess hall, but it was obvious Gari had something more urgent to discuss.

"Did you read Oswald Chambers today?" she asked excitedly.

"Yes," I said, not mentioning that I'd been reading it all night.

"Wasn't it *amazing*?" she continued.

I paused, recalling the topic of the reading. *Something about closer intimacy with Jesus.*

"Well, I thought it was *good*," I said slowly, "but not *amazing*."

She sounded surprised. "Are you *kidding*? Nothing's ever been a closer fit for what we needed!"

I was baffled.

As it turned out, Gari was right—though for some reason she'd read the November 7 entry instead of the one for January 7. But to Gari, it was no mistake. The Lord had led her to the "wrong" reading to find the right message for us.

In that light, it *was* astounding:

November 7

The Undetected Sacredness of Circumstances

"All things work together for good to them that love God."
Romans 8:28

The circumstances of a saint's life are ordained of God. In the life of a saint there is no such thing as chance. God by His providence brings you into circumstances that you cannot understand at all, but the Spirit of God understands. God is bringing you into places and among people and into conditions in order that the intercession of the Spirit in you may take a particular line. Never put your hand in front of the circumstances and say—"I am going to be my own providence here; I must watch this, and guard that." All your circumstances are in the hand

of God, therefore never think it strange concerning
the circumstances you are in.[2]

Had Gari mistakenly read the wrong devotion? We didn't
think so. It seemed to be another whisper from God.

It was exactly what I needed, in fact. I would keep reading
it over and over at night, just before stepping on the metal
chair and climbing onto my bunk.

Was it distraction therapy? Definitely. But the message also
brought me peace. I needed to remember that the circumstances of my life were in God's hands—and that I was too.

It had been a busy day. That night I took out my little
journal again and made a list of what I'd done:

JANUARY 7: *Up at 6:00 a.m. Great day. Much*
better. Went to the dentist. What a joke. Not much
of a checkup. Went outside for one hour to walk in a
circle. Talked to Andy, Ashley, and Gari today. Met
Tim and Mike at Bible study. Nuggets game came on
radio. Very weird thinking I'm not the chaplain. Wrote
letters. Read. Still a little tired. Very confused. Lots of
information and don't want to break a rule.

The Grind

The next couple of days saw the beginnings of routines, of
trying to get used to prison life.

There was a lot to get used to, starting with my claustrophobia. For me, living in a cell the size of a broom closet was worse than being jammed in the window seat on the last row of a packed airplane. I kept looking out the miniature front window or out the tiny glass-block back window to maintain my sanity. I couldn't live without a perspective beyond the tight—and tightening—four walls around me.

It was also a relief to get outside and "exercise." They'd send us out in small groups since there was so little space, and I'd think, *Ah! Air!*

But then I'd realize, *I'm going in a little circle here. This is a pretty pathetic bottom I'm hitting.*

I wasn't the only one who suffered the effects of lockdown, of course. Doors to and from the cellblock were closed and locked 24/7, and at night the cells themselves would lock. A "lockdown situation" would happen in case of a riot or escape; guards would run around with guns, and inmates weren't supposed to move.

Sometimes, as a result of being shut in so much, guys would really get crazy and scream. Others would carry on conversations from cell to cell, mostly for sanity's sake. The only remedy for me, at least at night, was standing by the dim light of the door and reading until I felt so tired that I could lie on my bed and try to sleep.

Most of the time, though, sleep didn't come. And when it did, it was never private, peaceful, or comfortable. Guards were banging around with their rings of giant keys, doing head counts in the middle of the night; inmates were yelling throughout the cellblock.

I wished I had a fan or a white noise machine next to my head, but devices like that weren't allowed. So, like most of the other inmates, I slept only about every third night. And that's just because I was exhausted.

I supposed the longer I was there, the more I might adjust to it.

I hoped I'd never have the chance to find out.

JANUARY 8: *Looked at picture of my family for the first time and cried. Twenty inches of snow last night. Much better sleep. . . . Outside walk today was great. Wrote to church. . . . Talked to Gari, Ashley, and Andy. My gold nugget today was the strength in Gari's voice.*

JANUARY 9: *Up at 6:10 a.m. today. Banana for breakfast. Called Lana. . . . No one there. Visited family tonight for three hours. Went outside for exercise in courtyard. John in commissary helped me out. Gave me toothpaste and deodorant and shoes that fit. Had a great visit with the family. Ashley and Gari are beautiful and soft. Andy looked big and strong. I could tell Andy thought I'd be mad about his algebra grade. I couldn't care less. He's great. I'm okay today. Feeling like I'm in God's will. Sharing with a few guys.*

The daily grind of prison life would occasionally be interrupted by God's intervention.

I'd spent five nights alone with "silent Sam," my cellmate.

A couple of guys had told me, "Sorry you're in with the biggest nut in the building."

But on the fifth day an inmate named David took pity on me. "In case you're stuck here for a while, you don't want to live with this guy," he said. "So pick up your stuff and follow me."

I frowned. "Are we able to just move around?"

"No," he said. "But I asked the guard, and he approved it."

Still a little apprehensive, I decided to go. I figured I was trading up because David was an ex-Marine, the cellblock barber—and all in all, a pretty normal-looking guy.

When we got to David's cell, he said, "Plus, I have a gift for you."

He handed me a plastic fork—a full-sized one! It was at least twice the size of the version I'd been issued and had been trying to eat with, the one that looked like it came from a doll set.

I didn't know how he got it, and didn't ask. I'd seen a few other inmates who brought them to the mess hall, so I figured he wasn't breaking any rules. I couldn't have received a better cell-warming present. The food didn't improve, but it did make eating easier.

Before long David told me the story of why he'd gone to prison—at least his version. His wife had needed surgery, and it would cost $7,500 he didn't have. He taped some highway flares together and went to the drive-up window of a bank.

Setting the flares in the tray, he said to the lady at the window, "This is a bomb. If you don't put $7,500 in there, I'm going to set it off."

So she put $7,500 in—and pushed the alarm button. David pulled the tray back. After placing the money and the flares in the front seat of the car, he drove off.

A mile down the road the police pulled him over. End of story.

I didn't know what kind of training David had received to cut hair, but for everyone's sake, I hoped he was a better barber—and cellmate—than he was a bank robber.

JANUARY 11: *Very tired today. Very lonely, mad about being here. Moved rooms today at 10:00. David is a great guy. Visit from Gari and the kids from 1:00–3:00 today. Very lonely tonight and very angry I'm here. My first weekend feels awful. I don't belong here, but everyone here says the same thing. I've started to sit on the steps and pray for every guy in here by name.*

JANUARY 12: *Little bit better today. Started crying when Nuggets game came on. Missed Andy today. Slept a little better. Tomorrow is going to be a good day. I see my family.*

Optimistic one minute, crying the next. My feelings, especially during the first week of prison, were confused—and confusing.

For most of that week I was hyperalert, fearing the worst, trying to be a tough guy, ready to fight.

If anybody wants to bring anything my way, I thought, *bring it on! I'll defend myself.*

I wasn't used to feeling that way. I'd been in a few fights in my life, but hadn't considered myself a fighter. Athletics had taught me to do battle in a different way—to win a contest. But it had never been mortal combat.

Now, though, it might be. I'd walked in fearful but determined, broken but ready to pounce. After several days of keeping my threat level too high, I knew I had to dial it back.

As Julie had warned me in the Cold Room, being hypersensitive and overreacting would only cause me trouble. Being anxious about anyone coming my direction would just make things worse for myself.

Still, I'd never faced anything this dangerous.

So far I hadn't made much progress in trusting God with my safety. I was so fresh in the system I didn't know that if I got into a fight, no questions would be asked; they'd simply add a year or two to my sentence and send me "deeper into the system."

Once I found that out, I backed off being overly vigilant and belligerent. Resistance, I learned, was futile.

I continued to believe that I was never going home, that this was my new life, but I also thought, *God's in control.*

So could I blame God for my predicament?

I didn't think so. I believed that if I decided to drive 120 miles per hour, crash my car, and kill myself, I couldn't fault God for not intervening and saving my life. He'd already intervened when He'd given me a brain. It wasn't His fault if I hadn't used it.

I'd usually taken my fair share of responsibility for losing a game or making a bad business decision. In this case I thought, *For my contribution to this, I take full blame.* I'd been too reckless, too aggressive, too impressed with myself.

So I wasn't angry with God. I was thankful that He was in control. I wasn't about to dump my faith and everything I'd believed in all those years since receiving Christ. If anything, I was going to cling more dearly to Him.

That didn't mean I was never frustrated with my situation. Occasionally I'd mentally run through all the unfairness I thought I'd seen in the legal proceedings. But if I was angry, I directed the emotion toward myself, not God.

I had done something that was permanently going to affect my future and my family.

On the cellblock steps or on my bunk, I'd think, *Here I sit. Nobody did it but me.*

No wonder I cried so much.

A Step Up

On January 13, one week after arriving at the Detention Center, I climbed out of my bunk at 6:00 a.m. and performed the job I signed up for. It was the only one available at the time—cleaning the showers. Somebody told me I'd better sign up for a job to keep from getting bored—though sanitizing showers while inhaling a sharp odor of sweat and disinfectant could hold my interest for only so long.

It gave me a chance, though, to think about how much I wanted to get out of the hard-core prison I was in and over to Camp Englewood. I was still being strip-searched on the nights my family visited, and my claustrophobia was suffocating. It was all too intense. I'd been told I might be in the Detention Center for a month, and after just a week I wasn't sure I could take it anymore.

Yet something odd had started happening the night before. I had the overwhelming feeling that things were about to change.

I began thinking, *Okay, we're done with this phase. You're moving on tomorrow.*

I had no reason to think that, but the thought just grew stronger. With it came a sense of God's peace—a peace that can't be explained but is nonetheless real.

The feeling was still strong when, after breakfast, I went back to my bunk to read. It was so strong, in fact, that I opened the door to my cell, thinking, *I need to leave this open so I can hear the guard's voice.*

Picking up the pen again, I wrote in my journal,

JANUARY 13: *I've made it one week. Got up today at 6:00 a.m. and cleaned all the showers. Feel like I'm moving to camp soon. Why? Because my family will be better if I do. Feels weird to be here. I can't explain it. Ate very little breakfast. I miss my family. Everything else is okay here. I've a real peace that I'm going to camp today. It's like God has told me . . .*

Within 15 minutes the guard yelled, "Mitchell, get your stuff! You're moving to the camp!"

Sweeter words I'd never heard.

Pulse quickening, I started packing my belongings. I still had the plastic trash bag, and it didn't take long to stuff everything in it.

I was excited—and relieved.

Yes, I'd still be in prison. But I knew everyone in our family would feel a little better about my surroundings.

The Bureau of Prisons could have left me in the Detention Center for a long time. I was, after all, just a number. But a bed had opened at the camp.

I was moving up—or so I hoped.

My travel time from the Detention Center to Camp Englewood was only a few minutes. They were both part of the same federal prison facility.

They were the same color, too—that pinkish-tan Colorado granite look. But there the external similarities ended. Instead of being a forbidding fortress like the Detention Center, the camp resembled a collection of unassuming army barracks or farm buildings. And unlike the Detention Center, the camp wasn't surrounded by rolls of razor wire. It was still prison, but the minimum-security kind.

The word "camp" didn't seem to describe it, though. It didn't look like a concentration camp. And it certainly wasn't a recreational summer camp or even a campground in the woods. In fact, there were practically no trees to be seen. Like much of Colorado, the scene was nearly desertlike.

After checking in, I saw the first advantage of my move. I was trading a six-by-nine-foot living space for an eleven-by-thirteen one. It wasn't called a cell, either. It was a *room*.

Not that there was *much* room, since these new quarters often housed at least four inmates. But I breathed a sigh of relief that my claustrophobia might be more bearable.

On the other hand, I quickly learned that there were new challenges.

On the first day, a few of the white guys told me to avoid any contact with "the blacks." They said, "We just don't get along with any of them, so keep your distance."

I shook my head. "Sorry, fellas. That's not who I am, and that's not how I treat people."

I knew I wasn't perfect when it came to prejudice, of course. I'd definitely noticed that the man who'd demanded my T-shirt when I'd walked into the cellblock was an African-American. Like many white guys, I'd probably made assumptions that left me feeling more intimidated because of it. But I'd been taught—especially by my dad—to treat people equally. And I'd spent four years in college sports and two years in pro baseball living, eating, and traveling with men of other races. I believed that, at their core, they were just like me.

Racial divisions had been obvious in the Detention Center, so I doubted the camp was worse. Still, I would be here a lot longer. I was determined not to show fear, and to be friendly with everybody.

So I told the white guys who'd just advised me to avoid "the blacks," "If I have to do something out of the ordinary to befriend everybody here because you guys have created a rift between whites and blacks, I'm gonna do it."

They warned me specifically about a guy named Earl who "runs the weight room and is mean as a hornet."

Naturally, I looked for Earl first.

I found him that afternoon in the weight room. Not surprisingly, he looked like a professional body builder. He was about six feet tall, and his arms were huge. He scowled at me. Judging from the lines on his face, he seemed to have had a lot of experience frowning.

I'd given him plenty to frown at. Since my arms were more suited for basketball than bench-pressing, I must have looked like a complete fool. I deliberately rolled my sleeves up to my shoulders, exposing my almost nonexistent biceps. Now I approached him and said, "Earl, I hear you run the weight room. And I want you to know—I'm comin' after you!"

He took one look at my pencil arms and broke into a smile. "You've got a problem," he said. "And I can help you."

We both laughed, then talked a few more minutes. The ice was broken, and I could tell we were on our way to a friendship. I valued that, and hoped his acceptance of me would also become a stamp of approval to other African-American inmates.

I didn't know whether the white inmates who warned me about Earl thought I was okay or not. But I knew 98 other sets of eyes were watching me, and I wanted to set a good example if I could.

Besides, my arms really *were* embarrassing. Earl was going to help me—maybe in more ways than one.

The System

My first evening at camp turned out to be a night to remember—for our whole family.

It started at dinner. No trays were thrown in anyone's face, but the incident proved even more disturbing to me.

Soon after I sat down at a table in the mess hall, a wiry—and wired—inmate sat across from me. Rick seemed fidgety, excitable, a fast-talking Type A car salesman.

"We all know that [the banker] screwed you because we've read about it in the paper," he said. "So I was wondering if you're going to try to kill him."

What?

It was clear the guy wasn't kidding. He really assumed I was the kind of person who might hire somebody to murder an enemy on the outside.

Conflicting emotions—hurt, sadness, anger—washed over me.

It turned my stomach to think that I'd sunk so low he could ask such a question. It frustrated me to know that he was right about what the banker had done. It shamed me to be reminded that, even though God was in control and had me in His hands, I'd made a real mess of things for myself, my family, and my friends.

Trying to think of a response, I found angry questions

flashing through my mind. How could I have been so careless seven years ago? Why was risk so attractive to me? Had I thought it was a sign of courage or intelligence to make decisions so quickly? Was I just a smart-mouthed, undisciplined jerk who deserved to be in prison?

Finally I responded to Rick: "No, I would never even consider that. I've got enough problems as it is."

With that, I picked up my tray and stepped away from the table.

I didn't want to face questions like that. I didn't like that others here seemed to know so much about me. How much more had they heard? Could they use that information against me?

After that encounter I rarely stayed in the mess hall longer than 10 minutes per meal.

It was beginning to look like camp wasn't the solution to my problems after all.

After dinner, Gari and Ashley and Andy came to visit. They were glad I'd moved out of the Detention Center and into the camp. But soon all of us were reminded that we were still at the mercy of the system.

We were sitting in the visitation room when a couple of the other visitors apparently wandered into a restricted area. Officer Dawson—a skinny little guard who could have been Barney Fife's twin—jumped to his feet. Angrily he grabbed the frightened visitors and yanked them back to the proper place.

But that wasn't enough for him. He made a sign and

taped it to the door—even though spelling was obviously not his strong suit:

NO VISSERTERS BEYOND THIS POYNT

I couldn't believe he wasn't joking. Turning to a seasoned inmate, I kept my voice low as I asked, "Is this guy for real?"

The inmate nodded. "And he is in charge of your life while you're here."

I could understand that the guards were trained to react quickly and were often harsh with inmates. But some treated even visitors with disrespect, as if family and friends came to take part in some covert action to overturn the whole system. And almost daily I'd see a guard change or randomly enforce a regulation just to inconvenience or embarrass an inmate. Following the rules, which I was committed to doing, became like trying to pick a winning lottery number.

So I learned to do my best, say "Yes, sir," a lot, and pretend that whatever the guards threw at me made perfect sense. I was also learning never to ask why, because the answer was always, "It is what it is because, for today, that's the rule. So follow it or find yourself in even more trouble!"

Officer Dawson reminded me that some guards were worse than others. A squirrelly little Barney Fife who thought wearing a badge made him a world cop was funny. But as an inmate, being under the authority of someone who loved power and selectively enforced the rules could be life-threatening. I made a mental note to watch my step even more carefully.

After our visit, Gari and the kids returned to our van in the parking lot—only to find the keys were locked inside. She had to return to the office for help, another complication and embarrassment she didn't need.

I knew it reflected the stress I was causing her. She was disoriented; no wonder she couldn't keep track of everything. Even visiting was scary; they scrutinized you, analyzed what you were wearing. I felt awful for her, thinking, *I have messed things up so thoroughly here, my wife can't keep her car keys straight.*

Like so many things, it was my fault.

God Shows Up

As if my first evening at Camp Englewood hadn't been eventful enough, I discovered that I arrived just in time for a rare occurrence: a concert.

More amazingly, one of the singers was a friend of mine— Janet Choice, a great performer from our church.

I was seated with most of the inmates in the mess hall when Janet and her group entered. To my pleasant surprise, she immediately spotted me and came over to give me a big hug and a kiss on the cheek! Whether the guards approved, I didn't know—or care.

It was wonderful to see her. Even better, though, was that all those inmates saw me get a kiss from a woman who was beautiful—and black.

I could practically hear the other prisoners thinking, *Who is the new guy getting the love from our guest singer?* At least some of the African-American inmates had to be thinking, *He must be okay, because she's one of us and she's kissing him.*

Without knowing it, Janet had given me a priceless gift. Between that kiss and my friendship with Earl from the weight room, it was going to be a lot easier to be accepted by "the brothers."

God seemed to be saying, "I'm going to solve any problem you might have with the black inmates—even before there *is* a problem." Unlike the white guys who warned me to stay away from the black guys, God apparently thought getting along was a good idea.

Earl and Janet had helped me adjust to my new life at Camp Englewood with just the right touch of grace. And God had whispered again that He was in charge—and knew what I was facing.

That night I slept in my new bed—new to me, anyway—the top bunk in my new room.

In the bunk below was Manny, a friendly guy about six foot one, 180 pounds. So far he'd been kind and soft-spoken. Everybody seemed to like him.

In the middle of the night, a searing pain in my leg woke me. It wasn't the first muscle cramp I ever had; all I could do was hold on until it passed.

Groaning, I grabbed my leg and waited. After an hour or so the pain faded. I sighed wearily and eventually fell back to sleep.

The next morning Manny told me he had to wrestle with his conscience during the night.

"I heard you up there," he said, "and I made a move to help you. But then I thought to myself, *You know what? If I make a move to help this new guy and he dies, I got problems.* So I just went back to sleep. But I'm glad to see you're okay this morning."

I couldn't blame Manny for thinking that way. As he knew—and as I was learning—the system wasn't set up for Good Samaritans. He really was a nice guy, but he couldn't change that in prison, no good deed goes unpunished.

After my euphoria over getting out of the Detention Center, Manny's words brought me back to reality. *Other than God, no one here is going to help me.*

My first 20 hours or so in prison camp had brought a few promising developments. Generally speaking, though, my feelings of relief had lasted about a day.

And I had many more days to go.

Gari's Story

The morning of Bo's first full day in prison, I woke up and made my hot tea—then sat down to read from the Bible and the Oswald Chambers devotional *My Utmost for His Highest*.

Bo and I simply called the book "Oswald." We treasured it because it was filled with wisdom and always drew us closer to God.

When I opened "Oswald" for that day, what I read blew

me away. It seemed God was speaking to me through the printed word—much as He'd done through Psalm 66 the night before.

I couldn't wait to share it with someone. Phoning Helen Dye, I asked, "Have you read 'Oswald' today? Can you believe what it says? It's amazing! I can't wait to share it with Bo!"

Breathlessly I read on and on through the devotional reading. Helen opened her copy and tried to follow along.

Finally she interrupted. "Gari, I don't think I am reading what you are reading—so could you tell me what date you are on?"

"Well," I said confidently, "it's November 7th."

At the time, this made total sense to me. No doubt Helen thought I was a little crazy, because the day's date was *January 7*.

In her sweet, patient voice, she asked, "Why don't you read me what you see?"

I did. It was all about Romans 8:28, and how God would work all things—even hard times—together for good. It was the perfect reminder that our circumstances were in His hands.

When the phone rang around 10:00 that morning and a voice asked whether I'd accept a collect call from the prison, I had to tell Bo right away about this teaching and how I'd been directed to read it. It meant so much to know God's hand was in everything and to understand that He knew exactly where Bo was and why.

Both of us would continue to read that devotion and Romans 8:28 over and over. We'd known God was always there, but found that at our most desperate hour we were intently listening and looking for Him—coming to know Him at a deeper level than ever.

We were clinging to any encouraging word from God—and others. During Bo's first week in prison, our friend Dr. James Dobson wrote us this understanding note:

> *I'm sure there is nothing I can say that will remove the pain you are feeling right now over Bo's situation, but I wanted to take a minute to let you know that you are not alone, that we sympathize deeply with what you are going through, and that we care about you!*
>
> *Of course, it's tragic and unfair that Bo has to go to prison, and I'm sure at this point it makes no sense at all to those who know him—and especially to you and the family. But the Lord never said that life would be fair or that we would always understand the circumstances of our lives; He simply asks us to follow Him, to do our best to obey, and to trust Him with the results. I know that Bo has tried to live this way, and he's been an inspiration to many. The fact that he's going to prison unjustly cannot and does not detract from that. I believe that if you've earnestly brought it all before the Lord, and this trial still happens, then He has a purpose in it all.*

"Oswald" couldn't have said it better himself.

CHAPTER 7

PRISON CAMP

IF THE DETENTION CENTER had been like a heart attack, Camp Englewood was more like quadruple bypass surgery. Better, but still bad.

There were plenty of reasons to call it *prison* camp, as Gari and I were finding out. The road ahead looked long, dangerous, and humiliating. We couldn't help longing for more assurance from God that He was in control. We'd heard some of His "whispers," but Gari prayed for a specific message.

On January 14, just a day after I moved to Camp Englewood, God sent it.

When the phone rang at our house that day, my sister Lana's husband, Charlie, was on the line with an amazing story. Gari relayed it to me, and later Charlie wrote it in a letter he sent my way:

> *I was awakened in the middle of the night by a message . . . "Philippians 1:13. . . . This is for Bo, and he needs to hear this." No sound effects, light show, or any other significant features. I wouldn't even say it was a voice except for the fact that it wasn't anything visual or written and it was not an original thought; it definitely came from some source outside my own head. It was like I heard it. At any rate, it takes quite a bit to wake me up, and usually I can shrug something off [as] a distraction and go back to sleep without any trouble. This time was different. I was wide awake and got a Bible and was astonished when I read the verse.*

This was what my brother-in-law, a man not given to visions or even to memorizing Scripture, found when he looked up Philippians 1:13: "As a result, it has become clear throughout the whole palace guard and to everyone else that I am in chains for Christ."

His letter continued,

> *I had never before nor since dreamt of a specific Bible verse but could imagine the possibility of that happening. However, for my brain to randomly pick a verse out of thin air and be so appropriate to your*

situation is beyond the laws of probability. It was
obvious to me that it was supernatural.

To us, this was God saying, "I'm in control. I've got this. This isn't a catastrophic accident; it's part of My plan. I'm already at work here."

That night I wrote in my journal:

JANUARY 14: *Slept poorly, but it feels much better.*
Walked four miles today. Charlie had a word from God.
Phil. 1:13. He said he was awakened at 3:00 in the
morning. WOW! Lana was praying I'd go to camp at
the exact time I was called. My roommate and some of
the other guys were sad I was leaving the jail. It's been
a good day, but the reality of being here for this year is
setting in.

That reality wasn't pretty. I quickly discovered that if such a thing as a "white-collar country club" prison camp existed, I hadn't received an invitation.

The impossibility of getting a decent night's sleep continued. The guards, clomping around in heavy boots and jangling their rings of oversized keys, did round-the-clock counts to make sure no one had escaped. That included bed checks at 10:00 p.m., 3:00 a.m., and 5:00 a.m.

They had to see skin to know that the lump in the bunk wasn't just a pillow. Since I slept with a blanket over my head to minimize the noise, they'd tug on it to see my arm or leg and touch me. It was like setting off three alarm clocks every night, and like many other inmates I was in a constant state of exhaustion.

One of my new roommates thought he had a solution. Zack claimed to have read a rule saying that if you were awakened by a guard and slugged him, you couldn't be held responsible for your "involuntary" action. So he said, "I'm tired of this touching Bo and waking him up. I'm gonna lie here awake tonight 'til the first bed check. And I'm gonna slug the guard."

Fortunately, we talked him out of it.

Food continued to be a problem too. It wasn't just that there was never a piece of meat, chicken, or fish. It wasn't only that the food was low quality, unvaried, and poorly prepared, either.

Sometimes there were worms in it.

They weren't writhing. Mostly they were cooked into the green beans. The worst part was that the guys who served the food thought it was hilarious.

Sometimes birds got into the food before it reached the kitchen. One day I watched as a food truck pulled up before being unloaded. The wind had blown the tarp back, and about 20 birds were pecking holes in our breakfast.

That was the day I decided not to have any more of those so-called sweet rolls.

In fact, I started avoiding the mess hall whenever I could. In my locker I stashed a jar of peanut butter and a loaf of bread—which I bought in the commissary—and made myself a sandwich for lunch nearly every day. Just peanut butter, no jelly.

It was no wonder, then, that I lost 36 pounds in prison—going from a slightly overweight 212 to a slightly underweight 176. The combination of very bad food and a lot of time to exercise was the formula for what I came to call the Federal Prison Diet.

In terms of exercise, I averaged at least five miles a day of fast walking on the dirt track south of the rooms. Every weekday I walked three quick miles over the lunch break and another three or four after dinner before visitation started. On weekends I'd usually double that since I had more free time.

For the most part, I spent every spare moment on the track—thinking, praying, and moving fast. I'd quietly sing praise songs like "I Love You, Lord," "As the Deer Pants for the Water," and "There's Just Something About that Name." Sometimes I'd walk with a roommate.

Even on cold days I'd go for it. It wasn't the kind of exercise I was used to—treadmills at the athletic club. And it might not have seemed like much of an accomplishment. But at the moment it was all I had.

For an hour or so it looked like I might have the exercise of softball, too.

A few weeks after I moved to the camp, I was invited to play in a softball game. It didn't surprise me when I was one of the last to be chosen. No doubt the two captains took one look at me and decided they didn't want the old guy on their team. They didn't know I'd played pro baseball and still could compete, especially in a prison game.

Our team batted first. Even though they had me hitting near the bottom of the order, I still managed two home runs in the first inning and another in the second.

As I circled the bases, the guys were hooting and hollering. I was happy to show the younger bucks I still had it.

But soon things turned ugly. Our team was ahead by at least 12 runs and still batting when one captain screamed at the other, "You're a bum and you don't know how to pick a team!"

The second captain fired a vulgarity in the direction of the first. A few more guys joined in the insults. Before long the verbal battle turned physical, and the game became a brawl. Some inmates were rolling on the ground, throwing punches as the guards came running.

I shook my head. *No, this is a risk I'm not taking anymore.* It was the last time I played. From then on I'd stick to the solitude of the track.

New Normal

Sleeplessness, repulsive food, and limited exercise weren't the only problems we faced at Camp Englewood. Other routines in my "new normal" made it hard to get up each day.

One was my new job in the business office on the upper floor of the Federal Correctional Institute. Despite the impressive-sounding name, it was just another pinkish-tan concrete fortress that was part of the prison complex—a three-minute bus ride from the camp.

The business office occupied about 3,000 square feet. A few of the civilian employees, all 13 of them women between the ages of 30 and 50, had private offices. Inmates sat at desks in a common area. There were windows to look out of; the place was bright but definitely not cheerful. At breaks the four inmate employees were allowed to step outside and walk around a flagpole on a cul-de-sac.

For us, most workdays began with cleaning the office's toilets. We took turns. It was actually the most fulfilling part of my job; the humility of cleaning someone else's toilet seemed like a healthy way to start the day. It was hard to think too highly of myself when I had my face and hands in that porcelain bowl—a good position for a guy who'd had a longtime problem with pride.

The rest of the job, though, was demeaning. Even though the woman in charge of the office was hardworking and generally respected, the other bosses hovered over us, making sure we were doing *their* work and not interfering with their coffee breaks. It was like a prison within a prison.

My starting salary was 11 cents an hour. After two months of performing well, I got a raise—to 23 cents.

I saw a lot of waste in that office but was in no position to be a whistle-blower. All I could do was ponder it—along with the irony that after being sent to prison for bank fraud, within a month I was basically responsible for paying the bills.

JANUARY 27: *Started work today at the business office and could not make the memory typewriter work. Very tough day. Very long day. Had a great visit with the family last night. . . . Read a book on humility. Hope I understand it.*

The business office may have been irritating, but it wasn't life-threatening. The same couldn't be said of another aspect of prison: medical care.

Before I was assigned a job, I was told I couldn't do anything but scrub walls and floors until I had my head-to-toe physical. So three or four times a day during my first two weeks at camp people would ask, "Have you had your physical yet? Is it scheduled?"

When I said no, I was told, "Our physician's assistant is going to give you a full physical exam from the top of your head to the bottoms of your feet." Dreading what I assumed would be painstaking and painful, I was eager to get the thing over with.

Finally my time was scheduled. The P.A. was a short, plain woman who wore camouflage outfits every day. Apparently she was opposed to small talk and liked to flex her authority muscles.

Picking up a clipboard, she asked me, "Are you ready for the exam?"

"Yes," I said nervously.

"Okay, let's start with your head. How's your head feeling?"

"Fine," I replied.

She proceeded to ask me the same question about my face, teeth, neck—right on down my body.

That was it.

Not a touch, not a tongue depressor, not a blood pressure check, not a blood test. And certainly not the thing I'd feared the most—a proctologic exam. It was over in minutes.

I thought, *You have to be kidding me! We could have done this three weeks ago!*

As far as I could tell, this lady provided most of the prison's medical care. She seemed to spend most of her time on the firing range with the guards, testing her skills. I knew if I had a medical issue that required more than aspirin, I'd be in trouble.

Unfortunately, some inmates found themselves in exactly that position.

One was Alex, a tall, strong, likable man considered a representative of the prison's black community. He also had a lump in his neck the size of a golf ball.

He was told it was a tumor. But he wasn't allowed to leave on furlough to let a specialist find out whether it was cancerous.

I never found out what became of him.

Later another inmate told me about a prisoner who collapsed on the softball field. Since it was Sunday, the story went, the P.A. who'd "examined" me was called at home. She reportedly said, "Well, for today just put him up in his bunk and give him a couple of aspirin."

He died that day of a heart attack.

That explained why another inmate had told me: "Don't get sick in here, because no one cares."

Sick at Heart

One more unwelcome routine made prison life harder. It wasn't a physical problem. It did, however, involve my heart.

The problem was that I was crying every day. Not constantly, but once or twice. Something stupid or cruel or unbelievable would happen and I'd think, *What am I doing here with these people? It must mean I'm one of them.* That would trigger tears.

So would the sight of my family leaving after visitation. Or times when I felt lonely. Or not knowing what was happening to Gari and the kids while we were apart. Or frustration over the loss of freedom, or the inability to get a good night's sleep, or the difficulty of staying out of harm's way.

I didn't cry from fear or embarrassment. Most often I wept when I considered what I'd done to create this mess. *I've let everybody down*, I thought.

FEBRUARY 13: *Feel very sad today because I've been deserted by [a few] Christian friends. It seems they just won't or can't understand what has happened to me. I think about my mom and dad and how this would have killed them if they were still alive. I think about all the people I've disappointed, like my family. Andy's*

*hero and best friend has been put in prison. What a
thing for a junior in high school to have to endure. He's
strong, but I can't even imagine what he's had to go
through. The pain must be awful for Gari, Ashley, and
other people as well.*

One fellow inmate—a gray-haired, quick-witted physician who'd been convicted in a real estate scam—seemed to understand. Every so often Victor would tell me, half-jokingly, "Bo, it's not good to cry *every* single day in prison. It's looking bad to the other inmates."

Unfortunately, Dr. Vic didn't have a prescription for my condition.

Neither did I.

Friends and Foes

Along with new routines came new friends—and adversaries.

In the first category was Marv Morrison, one of my roommates. A dark-haired, middle-aged man with sincere, caring eyes, he was also a Christian. With his southern drawl and easy manner, he seemed to be everybody's friend. Marv and I walked and prayed a lot together on the track.

Somehow Marv had ended up with the camp's best job: running the little prison library. If he wanted to, he could prop up his feet and read the Bible for three hours a day. I envied him.

Another friend and fellow believer was Carl, who arrived

at camp several weeks after I did. He and I spent a lot of time on the track, too.

Still another buddy was an older man we called "Hap"—as in "happy." The nickname was pure irony, as the poor guy was too scared to be jovial. A rotund, soft-looking fellow, shy and quiet, he always looked like he was hanging on by his fingernails. Yet he was kind, trying to get along with everybody. A few of us tried to watch out for him, making sure he was okay.

Hap worked with me in the business office—another irony, since he'd been convicted of embezzlement. A small-town bank employee, he'd "borrowed" money for his children's tuition and paid it back years before being discovered—but had to go to jail anyway.

Finally, there was Mr. Swanson. Maybe "friend" wasn't the right word for him; after all, he was the camp administrator, like a warden. But more often than not, he seemed supportive of me and many others. A short, very slender African-American, he was a good leader—straight-shooting, no-nonsense. His empathy with the inmates was striking; sometimes it felt like he was the only person in camp pulling for us.

Then there were the other guys—those who were sometimes friends, sometimes something else.

Zack was one of those. He was the roommate who'd had the brilliant plan to slug a guard for waking me up.

A tall guy with an athletic build, Zack had been a successful salesman before prison. He was friendly, lighthearted—and a Christian.

But he was impulsive, wouldn't listen, and didn't take the rules seriously enough—which irritated the guards and endangered the rest of us.

Sometimes his rebellion was a small matter, like the day he had a red polo shirt smuggled in and wore it around for a morning—just to antagonize the guards. "Where'd you get that?" they finally growled. "Take it off!"

Zack ditched the shirt, but not the smuggling. He was one of several inmates who would order pizza and have it delivered during visitation hours near the trash can behind the mess hall. After everybody left, the smuggler would sneak out and get the pizza.

One night Zack asked, "What kind of pizza do y'all want tomorrow night?"

I said, "Somebody write down that Bo said, 'I want *no* pizza.' I don't want pizza. I want to go home. I want to see my family. I want to be done with this."

I didn't need any more trouble, certainly not over a slice of pizza. Did I think Zack was funny? No. Did he do this kind of thing all the time? Yes.

When Zack first came to the camp, he asked me for advice. I told him what Julie from the Cold Room had told me: "If you see it, you didn't see it; if you hear it, you didn't really hear it; mind your own business."

Later that night Zack returned to our room and told us

that the guys in his room were smoking. He told them there wouldn't be any smoking in their room.

"Zack, I just told you to mind your own business," I said. "Now you're already instructing these guys on whether they're smoking."

"I don't want them smoking."

"Well, we'll see you in a couple of weeks," I said. "Because you're going to The Hole tomorrow."

The Hole was like solitary confinement, but not quite as severe. It wasn't a dark, dank place where you'd lie in a fetal position in the corner. You sat in a room, alone, your food slid under the door. You couldn't have visitors or go to work. The Hole was in the Federal Correctional Institute, where I worked in the business office, and we'd heard about it from guys who'd been sent there.

Zack looked shocked. "Why am *I* going to The Hole?"

"Because I told you to keep your mouth shut," I said. "You don't think those guys are gonna wait for you to turn them in for smoking, do you? They're already turning *you* in. You'll be carted off tomorrow."

Next morning, leaving for work, I said to Zack, "See you in a few weeks." Sure enough, he was taken off to The Hole.

When Zack came back, camp administrator Mr. Swanson called me into his office. "Look," he said. "I know you're sick of your room being overcrowded. But if you don't take Zack in your room, I have to send him deeper in the system to another prison. Those guys will hurt him if he goes back to the room he was in. Will you take him?"

I sighed. "You leave me no choice."

So we were stuck with Zack. After having the population of our room reduced to "only" four guys for one day, we were back to five. We didn't celebrate.

Camp Englewood seemed full of guys like Zack—characters who could exist only on this foreign planet called prison.

Miguel, known as the camp tailor even though he had no particular qualifications—was a sloppy dresser. A chubby fellow, he was usually smiling—until his quick temper took over. After I'd been losing weight for a month on the Federal Prison Diet, I went to him for help with my wardrobe.

"Miguel," I said, "I'm tired of these pants being 10 inches too big around my waist. Can you fix these?"

"Yep. Thirty-five dollars."

I frowned. "Well, that's what I'd pay on the *outside* to have pants tailored."

"Yeah," he said. "Well, that's what you pay here, too. You're not on the outside, are you? You're on the inside."

Point taken; I paid him. He took one side of the pants, folded it over, and with two stitches created a rather awful-looking, lopsided pleat. I couldn't deny that I suddenly had pants that didn't fall down.

Miguel, on the other hand, must have decided he'd rather be on the outside. One night he hopped the fence. The guards claimed to have caught him and sent him "deeper into the system," but they hadn't. An ex-inmate later spotted him living in another state but didn't turn him in.

Then there was Ed, the meanest prisoner in the camp.

He had a tough-looking face, long hair, and was in jail for dangerous, scary stuff. He worked in the warehouse, where he stole every piece of fruit that came in. None of the guys in my room, or in the whole dorm, had ever seen a piece of fruit make it to the mess hall; Ed and his buddies in the warehouse had eaten them all.

About my second week in the camp, I was reading in my bunk before lights out. Suddenly Ed came in and put six bananas on my chest.

"Thought you might like some bananas," he said, and walked out.

My roommates were awed. "What'd you do for Ed to get bananas?"

I didn't know, but I could guess. Ed had been quite taken with the beauty of my daughter, Ashley, since he'd spotted her at visitation. He'd even started calling me Dad—his way of saying, "Soon as I get out of here, I'm marrying her." I guess he meant it as a compliment; I thought it was kind of amusing. It made Ashley cry, though. She found it extremely disturbing, and it caused her to have nightmares and become ill.

Soon Ed invited me to a party in his room. I went, and found myself surrounded by his friends—the meanest group of guys in camp. I was also surrounded by a whole spread of cheeses, three different kinds of cold cuts, and bread—no doubt all smuggled in.

I said, "No, thanks," and left.

They kept inviting me to their parties, but I always turned them down. It was nice to be included, though I wasn't sure what they liked about me. I figured it had something to do with the Lord.

Whatever the reason, I couldn't afford to break the rules about stealing food, smuggling pizza, or anything else. I didn't want to spend a single extra minute in prison.

Lifeline

If prison camp was a foreign planet, visitation and phone calls were my lifeline to Earth.

Gari and the kids continued to visit nearly every night and day. After years of trying too hard to do big things even at my family's expense, I found myself sitting across from them for hours each week with nothing to do but talk and just be together. In a way, prison was giving us a way to start over.

It was probably the first time the kids realized, *Hey, Dad's not bulletproof.* Ashley had decided to take the semester off from college, to stay home and help Gari and me.

"If this happened to me," she told Gari, "Dad would get an apartment next door so he could visit me every day. I want to be home. I can't be in Kansas when my heart is in Denver."

Ashley and I had struggled when she reached the teen years; often I'd been too controlling and overpowering. Now things were better because she could see how much I needed her. She even told me, "I feel like I can finally talk to you and we can be friends."

As for Andy, being apart was especially hard. At one point he told his mother and sister, "Don't expect much. I'm doing the best I can, but my best friend is in prison and when he gets out I'll be okay."

To me, he said, "Dad, I wish I could come in there with you." One night at visitation he even asked a guard if he could have a furlough to come *in* and stay with me overnight. The guard said no, of course, but my son's offer moved me more than I could say.

Gari and I began to grow closer too. Sometimes our visits were hard as we talked about issues in our marriage, or as it hit me anew how much pain my actions had caused her. But she stayed strong, and I was grateful she was feeling well enough to do all she needed to do, because I knew her health was far from normal. And amazingly, Gari could still find the funny in things, making us all laugh.

The other inmates noticed how often my family visited and how close we were. A few even said to me, "How do you get a family like yours?"

My answer was always, "It starts with Christ."

One person who tried to keep things light when my family visited was Dr. Vic—the inmate and physician who'd advised me not to cry every day. He'd stroll by our table in the visitation room—we always sat at the same one—and say, "You kids relax. They're down to one simple decision on your father—electric chair or lethal injection."

I thought it was funny.

Gari and the kids—not so much.

As the weeks passed, my list of approved visitors expanded to friends—a lot of them. Often visitation was the highlight of my day; afterward I'd write in my little fake-leather journal how things had gone. As the comments showed, my emotions were veering wildly from grief to elation and back again:

Best group visit we've ever had tonight. It was like a party, almost. Ashley and Andy and his friend Kyle. Gari, Ev and Helen Dye, and Bob Beltz . . .

Rainy today. Felt scary tonight sending my family home in the rain without me there to protect them.

Another great group visit tonight. Luis Villarreal, Dan Hendrick, Phil Irwin, Bob Beltz, Todd Eley, Gari and the kids. As hard as it might be to believe, we had a tremendous time.

Felt very sad today. I really miss my family. Andy went to spend time with Lana and Charlie. Is my faith weak? I feel very scared again. . . . Gari is home all alone. That makes me very sad.

Had a great two-hour visit today with Bill McCartney. We prayed and we talked about Christ and he shared a lot of Scriptures with me. Five times now in the last two weeks I forgot I was in prison. That is a great feeling.

Tough visit with Gari tonight. She cried big tears. I feel like I've let her down.

*Every time the family visits, we've been praying together.
Ashley's and Andy's prayers are so deep and so helpful to
me. It's great that we can talk to God in prayer.*

*I cried all night at visitation tonight. Then my friend
Todd Eley from the Nuggets came and pulled me out of
it. Gari is being so strong. She suggested Andy and I sit
in the corner for half an hour together just to be alone,
and for the longest time all we did was cry together.
Neither of us could say a word. Our hearts were
breaking . . .*

Fortunately, Andy and I were able to touch base nearly every
morning. I'd call him collect.

For him, it was a way to know I hadn't been harmed during the night. For me, it was reassurance that my family was
still there and Andy was still answering the phone. It was like
a breath of fresh air from the outside.

It was my link to a life I missed—and was hoping I would
get back to someday. Phone calls and visits weren't the only
way we stayed in touch. There were letters and greeting
cards, too.

The Mitchells were keeping the U.S. Postal Service in
business. Dozens of cards and letters flew back and forth
between my cramped, crowded room and our home address.
There were notes from me to Gari, from Gari to me, from
me to Ashley and Andy individually and together and vice
versa, and from me to the whole family.

Eventually the record holder would be Ashley, who sent me an incredible 100 letters.

As for Andy, his specialty was answering the phone, not writing notes. But he did send a few, once writing:

> *Just look at this situation as me kicking a field goal. It takes a man to deal with pressure, and to come through in the clutch. This is different than football, but I know you will be a man and stay strong. We love you, and no matter what happens, we will still love you.*

On at least one occasion I addressed a letter to the entire family. I had much to thank them for. And I did my best to be inspiring:

> *Dear Ash, Andy, and Gari—*
> *I get so much comfort every day just thinking about you three. Knowing that you have each other to lean on, and depend on for help, gives me a lot of help. You three are my hope for the future. The difficulties of these days apart from you are nothing compared to the dreams I have for our future!*
>   *No one could love his family more than I love you all. That is why this is so hard—our love is strong, and being apart like this is so unnatural. It just doesn't work for us. So all we can do is trust that God in us is strong and faithful and will see us through this—to the other side.*

*I'm praying more, and reading the Bible more, and
I'm closer to God than I've been in a long, long time.
I'll come out of here better than ever, and ready to help
you three more than I ever have. I'll miss you guys on
Tuesday and Wednesday, but it won't be long 'til I don't
have to miss you at all. You're the greatest!*

Dad

Not bad—for a man who couldn't stop crying every day.

Gari's Story

A few weeks after Bo went to prison, I began to understand
that the Lord had my husband's best interest in mind. God
had plucked him from his daily world and set him in a place
where people weren't calling him to ask for money, or to
find them a job, or create a ministry, or raise funds to fulfill
their dreams. For so long Bo had seemed to be the answer to
everyone's question: "Who can do this?" These requests had
become overwhelming, and Bo had a tough time saying no.

Apparently the Lord had rescued Bo and stashed him
in a spot where he could concentrate on God and his life.
I started calling prison Bo's "Enforced Spiritual Retreat." I
don't think he found that funny, but it helped both of us see
it all from a more positive perspective.

When Bo was sentenced, I'd started praying that the Lord
would give him a sign that God was in control of this whole
mess and had a plan for him. When his sister, Lana, called me

to say that her husband, Charlie, had something he wanted to tell me, I paid close attention. Lana and Charlie had been staying so close to us, writing and calling with encouragement and praying for all of us.

Lana was a strong Christian who'd studied Scripture for many years. Charlie knew Christ as his Savior but had never spent much time in the Bible. That's one reason his story about Philippians 1:13 was so amazing.

I was stunned by this vision; it was the sign I'd been praying for. I could tell Charlie and Lana were having trouble taking in this miracle—as was I. But the three of us knew it was a real message from God.

Soon our lives—Ashley's, Andy's, and mine—seemed to revolve around visiting Bo. We could see him on Wednesday, Thursday, and Friday nights from 5:30 to 8:30, and Saturdays and Sundays from 9:00 a.m. to 3:00 p.m. We almost never missed an opportunity to be with him.

Sometimes visitation could be funny—in a dark way. Without meaning to, Officer Dawson made sure of that.

One night someone had written a curse word on a Styrofoam cup in the visitation area. Officer Dawson was offended.

I told him I was too. "It was sophomoric," I said, "for someone to do that."

His eyes narrowed. It was a word he obviously had never heard. He seemed to think I was making fun of him. I remembered hearing that he'd left high school after tenth grade.

"The message on the cup was *silly*," I added hastily.

As soon as he heard that, he relaxed.

So did I. You just never knew what Officer Dawson might do.

There were about 20 people on Bo's approved visiting list. They could come any time they wanted during visiting hours. Others could be approved for one-time visits.

Often Bo had 10 or more visitors at a time. We had nothing to do but sit around, tell jokes and stories, visit, play cards, and have serious conversations—just being together. There was no TV, no radio, no distractions whatsoever. We had each other's full attention.

As Bo said, his "Enforced Spiritual Retreat" was the best of times and the worst of times. I felt that way too. For me the best part was time with Bo and the support of friends who visited in prison, called me often, brought food by the house, and helped financially. The worst part was the relentless stress and sadness.

Our despondency streamlined our routine. Andy would get up in the morning, talk to Bo on the phone, and go to school. I would wake up, and then Ashley and I would do whatever needed to be done in the house.

We all had this grief in our hearts the entire time. We didn't go to a movie; we didn't eat at a restaurant. We didn't do much of anything.

Ashley said later, "Mom, we didn't have *money* to do anything."

"Yeah," I said, "but we didn't *feel* like doing any of that anyway."

We missed Bo, who was usually the fun-bringer in our

family. He'd created a lot of good times for our kids. When Andy was four we'd taken car trips and seen big electrical towers along the highway. Bo had called those "giants" and made up stuff about them. When Ashley had a birthday party, she didn't want any adults there—but requested her dad's presence because he was so funny.

Now Andy stepped in, doing his best to keep our spirits up. He'd bring over his good friend Chad, and the two of them were like a comedy show. They kept us going.

I, on the other hand, had a survival technique nobody else seemed to find entertaining, especially the kids. I arranged and fluffed silk plants—fake greenery and flowers. It was just something I could do, a cheap hobby, a way to keep moving.

We tried to keep moving spiritually, too. We'd pray as a family when we saw Bo at camp. Bo and I continued to read "Oswald" every day and discuss what we found.

But that wasn't the only daily practice Bo had developed. As he said, he was crying at least once a day.

He just had a tender spirit and wore his emotions on his sleeve more than I did. I could keep my feelings hidden but that was difficult for Bo.

One day Bo gave me a message on a yellow sticky note:

Last night I was crying because it was one of the many times that I was overcome with how great you are, Gari, and how much your love and support mean to me. Ash and Andy have been just as supportive, and

I'm so grateful to you all!! I can't wait to get home and start returning to you the love you've given me.

I won't cry now—for a while.

Bo

I shouldn't have been surprised that he expressed his feelings with tears. I could remember how his dad had been the same way—weeping when the national anthem was played at baseball games.

In the beginning of our marriage Bo had cried about things like the first day one of our children went to first grade. But now it was different.

Now he was crying because his heart was broken.

CHAPTER 8

CHAINS AND MIRACLES

Since my first night at Camp Englewood, I hadn't been able to forget that my imprisonment wasn't just a legal matter. It was a spiritual one.

In fact, I saw a reminder of that almost every evening. It was a giant, glowing cross that comforted my whole family.

Known as the Mount Lindo Cross, it is the largest lighted cross in the United States. A landmark for countless people in the Denver area, it stands nearly 400 feet tall in the foothills of the Rocky Mountains—illuminated with bulbs that make it visible for miles.

It is part of the Mount Lindo Cemetery and Mausoleum. The property owner's father had wanted to be buried there, with a cross marking the spot. His wish was carried out—and the cross was positioned so his widow could view it from her house. The lights were first switched on in 1964—on Easter.[3]

It was an interesting history, but history wasn't on my mind when I looked at it.

Each night after visitation Gari and the kids would leave through the door to the west. I'd go out the door to the east, then walk 30 yards across the parking lot to my room at the camp. In that gap between the buildings, I would see the cross.

I couldn't miss it; it was big and bright and right in my face. It felt like I was living right under it. And in a way I was.

It was a guiding light, a symbol of what was going on with the family and with me. It seemed to say, *Things are under God's control, and you're here to learn some hard but necessary lessons.*

In a way, it lifted me above my circumstances. But it also reminded me how I'd ended up in those circumstances and dragged my family along.

So as I walked those 30 yards almost every night and looked up at the cross, the comfort of its presence mingled with my sadness.

Having a view of a famously huge cross wasn't the only visible evidence of spiritual things at Camp Englewood, of course. The prison had a part-time, volunteer chaplain who showed up on Sunday nights to lead chapel.

Unfortunately, that wasn't working too well.

I discovered that when I attended my first Sunday night

meeting. Out of a population of 100 inmates, there were only three of us—plus Chaplain Halsey.

He was slender and quiet. Discomfort, fear, and a lack of confidence seemed to be written all over his face.

For some reason he'd set up the four metal folding chairs facing each other—so close that we could feel each other's breath.

So here we were—Chaplain Halsey, me, and two of the toughest-looking guys I'd ever seen—practically nose to nose. And the chaplain asked us to sing "Jesus Loves Me."

I could see in the eyes of the other inmates that they were already looking for an escape route and mentally crossing next week's meeting off their calendar.

I thought, *Are we trying to make this as uncomfortable and awkward and unappealing as we possibly can?*

I didn't really want to get involved, to fix things. I was here to shut up and learn something, not to be a Christian leader. But I'd learned a few things about cultural relevancy at Denver Seminary, and couldn't help noticing how irrelevant the chaplain's approach seemed.

Well, I thought, *maybe I could help a little.* It seemed obvious why nobody was coming to these meetings.

So later I decided to ask the chaplain a question. I tried to be gentle. "You don't like doing this, do you?" I said.

There was a long pause. Finally he said, "You're right. I don't."

I had one more question, also gentle: "Why don't you do something else?"

He didn't answer right away. But apparently he took my suggestion to heart.

Within a month we had a new chaplain.

His name was Del. He was tall, wore glasses, and had a huge smile. A hearty soul with a great laugh, he exuded friendship and encouragement. He was comfortable and made us feel the same—unlike his predecessor.

The inmates who knew him loved him. Attendance at chapel more than quadrupled immediately. It helped that we talked him up to other inmates, but it was Del who attracted others with his care and his obvious interest in fulfilling his mission.

Even Del couldn't do it all; he was only there an hour and a half one night a week. But he made things more fun and more in line with who we were.

Still, it was discouraging to see so few of the overall prison population interested in spiritual things. Sunday night attendance topped out at around two dozen.

I knew that most inmates—like most people outside—had misplaced priorities. It always saddened me to see this demonstrated every day at dinnertime. That's when about 50 guys would gather in a hallway after everybody was accounted for in "standing count." A guard would yell, "All clear!" Then the guys would run full speed to the mess hall.

Since dinner usually tasted like dog food to me, I was always amazed that this group would sprint and shove to get there first. They never showed that kind of interest in chapel or in Prison Fellowship's Bible study on Tuesday nights.

If anyone needed to know what God had to say, it was

these 100 guys who'd gotten themselves into federal prison. But like their counterparts outside, they preferred the dog food the world had to offer. It was a pathetic snapshot of mankind that burned itself into my brain.

Hard Pressed

Prison life often seemed like a spiritual battle. At least it was reminiscent of a Bible passage:

> We are hard pressed on every side.
> 2 CORINTHIANS 4:8

Every day in prison, I felt threatened from all sides—by the prison system, by other inmates, by the judicial system, and by a few disloyal friends on the outside.

When it came to the prison system, the guards were constantly threatening to send you to The Hole if you messed up. Some seemed to make up rules and enforce others selectively. Seldom did I personally have a problem with a guard—but I felt threatened at all times because of the way I'd seen other inmates mistreated.

Such was the case with Leo. He was about my age, 42, short and bald and generally irritating. He held strong opinions, which he was always eager to express in a loud and squeaky voice.

Leo had been a lawyer on the outside. His specialty was defending drug dealers. He'd done it so well that the government had decided, "We're sick of you, so we're just going to put you in prison." At least that was how Leo told it.

One night an inmate who'd soon be leaving prison gave his transistor radio to another inmate. A guard got wind of this, and for some reason was taking issue with it.

A few of us watched as Leo stepped into the conversation. "I'm an attorney," he said. "And I don't think you're reading that rule the way it's written. Here's the way I think it's intended . . ."

"No," the guard said, scowling. "You're not an attorney. You're an inmate."

"Well, at the moment I'm an inmate," Leo argued. "But I'm also an attorney."

Steaming, the guard headed for Leo's room. "I'll show you you're not an attorney," he said.

The guard grabbed a bedsheet and unfolded it in the middle of the floor. Crashing and banging his way through the room, he emptied all the closets and cabinets. Then he took everything he'd collected and threw it in the middle of the sheet. Finally he bundled up the sheet like it was Santa Claus's bag and dragged it down the hall.

He threw the whole thing in the dumpster. Not just Leo's belongings, but all his roommates' stuff, too. It was all they had, and had taken months to accumulate from the commissary and wherever else they could scrounge it. Now it was gone.

The moral of the story was clear: "You may think you're a minister, attorney, husband, father—but what you really are is an inmate. A number. Nothing more. Don't get confused."

Another message the prison system seemed determined to communicate was even more threatening.

The rifle range was just 30 yards from the front door of the prison camp. We'd hear the cracking of gunfire frequently as the guards—and the physician's assistant—practiced.

Maybe there was a good reason for that. But we inmates thought it was a little strange. *Couldn't they put that somewhere off in the distance?* I wondered. *Or is this to remind us, "We've got guns and you don't"?*

Struck Down

Then there was the threat from a second direction—other inmates. My constant fear of violence wasn't unfounded.

I saw the truth of that firsthand in a heart-stopping incident about two months after coming to Camp Englewood.

It was evening, and a long line of inmates were waiting to make phone calls. There were only two pay phones for 100 prisoners. All calls had to be collect. Each person could have a 10-minute conversation.

But one guy, Kurt, had been on the phone for 40 minutes. Kurt had the inmates stacked up deep, and there was no sign that he was about to yield. Nobody seemed eager to make him, either; Kurt was about six foot four, overweight, arrogant, and not well-liked. Edgy and jumpy and dangerous-looking, he always talked too much.

I was next in line.

Another inmate, Anthony, was three or four people behind

me. He was skinny, about five foot six and 125 pounds. He looked like a college wrestler. Usually he seemed pretty cheerful, but not that night.

Finally Anthony decided he'd had enough. He stomped across the parking lot to the weight room in the mess hall, found a two-and-a-half pound weight, and put it in a white tube sock.

Walking back toward me down the hall, he swung the weighted sock like a weapon. I could see he'd done this before; he knew what he was doing.

I, on the other hand, had never faced a situation like this. My thoughts went into overdrive. *Now, outside of prison, you'd step out of line to stop him. "Anthony, don't do that. Kurt will be off the phone in a minute. You can have my spot in line. Don't make it worse for yourself."*

But this wasn't the outside. I remembered what Julie in the Cold Room had said, "You didn't see it. Keep your mouth shut. Mind your own business."

Only seconds remained before it would be too late. I should stop Anthony. This is not going to go well.

But I could guess the consequences if I tried to intervene. Besides being assaulted myself, I'd probably be punished for fighting. I—and my family—might be caught in the middle of a blood war or a court case between Kurt's and Anthony's relatives.

I told myself, *I'm not really seeing what I'm getting ready to see. I'm not going to be involved in an attempted murder.*

Anthony stepped around the corner toward the pay phone.

I stared as he swung, the weight burying itself in Kurt's forehead with a sickening thud. It looked as though Kurt's head had been split in half.

Within seconds, the hallway was soaked in blood. Some of us ran for towels, first for Kurt and then to clean up the blood before the guards could see it. Other inmates ran to find the guards—not to get help, but to score points by snitching.

Soon the guards came racing in. Kurt and Anthony were handcuffed and taken away—probably to The Hole. We assumed Kurt would get no medical attention—and probably would die anyway because his wound already looked fatal.

We never heard from either of them again, and I never heard anything about the incident after that. But I never forgot it, either—or its stark reminder that in prison, danger was always just a heartbeat away.

Perplexed

As for the judicial system, I'd felt hard pressed by it since the first day I'd been called by the FBI. Now it crossed my mind almost daily that the government could do whatever it wanted—and that I had little control of the situation. I stayed permanently concerned that an agent, prosecutor, or judge might pounce on me again from out of the blue.

Most of the time I kept my thoughts about justice to myself. But one day, after I'd been in the camp for a few months, I was invited to share them—with a panel of federal judges.

Camp administrator Mr. Swanson called me into his office

one afternoon and said, "Mitchell, I want you and Alex to speak to 13 federal judges who are touring the facility tomorrow."

I sank lower in my chair. If there was anything I didn't want to do, it was to risk the wrath of the judicial system. Finally I said, "I've only seen one federal judge in my life, and that didn't work out too well for me. So I think I'll pass on talking to 13 of them."

Mr. Swanson was a good guy, and I liked him a lot. But he was also in charge. "This is not a request," he said firmly. "It's an instruction as to what you'll be doing tomorrow."

I sighed. "Yes, sir. And what do you expect me to say?"

He explained that the judges would ask me and Alex questions, which we were to answer honestly.

I wasn't sure why Mr. Swanson chose us. Alex was articulate, so maybe he figured we would be good spokesmen. But it put me in a bad place—not just taking a chance that I'd displease a bunch of judges, but that other inmates might see me as a snitch or a pet of the guards. Prison was an awkward place to be when 99 other guys began to wonder what you were up to.

But I didn't have a choice. I decided to be honest and shoot from the hip—so to speak.

Next day a couple of guards took Alex and me into a small room adjacent to Mr. Swanson's office. My stomach was churning.

The guards led us to the front of the room, where we faced a seated group of 13 professional-looking people with serious expressions. About one-third were women. Both genders seemed uncomfortable, as if this was their first time in a prison.

I felt like a monkey on display at the zoo. I was even more nervous when I saw the five guards standing at attention against the wall. This would be a chance to make *a lot* of enemies.

Our conversation began when I was asked to describe prison life. I said that in my opinion they, as part of the judicial system, had little if any idea how the Bureau of Prisons actually worked. I told them that the sentences they gave inmates were powerful enough; they could soften their method of delivery for the benefit of our families and still accomplish their goal.

"The weight of your words is enough," I said. "You don't have to deliver such heavy words with such a harsh method. It is already devastating to the families involved."

When I said that, I noticed one of the female judges quickly putting on her sunglasses to hide the fact that she was starting to cry.

It made me think, *The judicial system really doesn't know what prison feels like. All they know is that they're doling out sentences to lawbreakers.*

Trying not to look at the line of uniformed figures along the wall, I also told the judges that they were under the illusion that the guards were here to serve and even to help the inmates. In fact, I said, they were here to intimidate.

When it was over, I knew nothing had changed.

Except that I'd given the system one more reason to make sure I'd never escape its grasp.

Persecuted

Lastly, I felt oppressed by people on the outside who ignored me and my family—or worse.

Ninety-nine percent of our friends and family members supported us completely and were of great help to us. But in a few cases, Gari and I felt attacked by those who chose to toss a little more dirt on our graves.

One local businessman wrote me a note, admitting, "In an effort to hurt you more, while you were gone I said things about you that were not true."

I wasn't sure why he did that, but it hurt us deeply as he verbally tore into me, my family, and our reputations.

So I felt oppressed and attacked from all four sides—the prison system, the inmates, the judicial system, and rumors started by a few disloyal friends. But I hoped to share the apostle Paul's experience, the one he described in the rest of that 2 Corinthians passage: "We are hard pressed on every side, but not crushed; perplexed, but not in despair; perse-cuted, but not abandoned; struck down, but not destroyed" (2 Corinthians 4:8-9).

With all this oppression, it often seemed I was in chains.

The Bible verse my brother-in-law had dreamed of appeared to confirm that I was "in chains for Christ." Gari saw me in a different kind of bondage, as her note had revealed: "I sense God breaking the chains that have bound you daily. But there is great pain, because our chains are in us deep and pulling them away hurts."

RIGHT: Bo Mitchell and Gari Geddes at their wedding on May 23, 1971.

BELOW: Gari's family in 1966. Back row (L to R): Gari and her older brother, Jim; middle row: Gari's parents, Alice and Jim; front row: Ali and Susan.

RIGHT: The Mitchell family in 1958 (L to R): Margaret, Lana, Bo, and Dale. Standing is Bo's older brother, Dale Jr.

DALE MITCHELL
outfielder CLEVELAND INDIANS

Bo's father, Dale Mitchell, played for the Cleveland Indians from 1946 to 1956, striking out only 119 times in 3,984 career at-bats.

ABOVE: Dale on a TOPPS baseball card.

RIGHT: Dale warming up before an Indians game. His career batting average was .312.

ABOVE: Bo in 1972 playing pro ball for the St. Petersburg Cardinals.

RIGHT: Bo made headlines as a University of Colorado basketball player.

NEXT PAGE: Signed by Yankees catcher Yogi Berra, Dodgers pinch hitter Dale Mitchell, and Yankees pitcher Don Larsen, this photo captures Larsen's final pitch to Bo's father during the perfect game of the 1956 World Series. Bo was in the stands, watching his father become part of baseball history as he struck out.

Yogi Berra
Dale Mitchell
Don Larsen

Catcher
Last Batter
Pitcher

Yankees · Dodgers

WORLD SERIES / 1956

"The Last Pitch"
October 8, 1956

THE ONLY PERFECT GAME IN WORLD SERIES HISTORY

Family Life: Andy, Gari, Bo, and Ashley in 1986; Ashley and Andy as toddlers; Gari with infant Ashley in 1973; Bo with Ashley in 1988.

L to R: Cherry Hills Community Church cofounders Barb and Jim Dixon, Gari and Bo, and Bob and Allison Beltz.

LEFT: Cherry Hills Community Church soon outgrew the space in its first building.

BELOW: One of the earliest Sunday services.

CLOCKWISE: The Mount Lindo cross, viewed from the prison where Bo was incarcerated, offered hope to Bo and his family; the halfway house, Bo's final stop before freedom; Bo, Andy, and Gari during a brief welcome home before Bo finished his sentence at the halfway house; the Federal Detention Center, Bo's first stop during his prison ordeal.

LEFT:
Bo and Gari with President George Bush and his wife, Laura, in happier days following Bo's time in prison.

RIGHT: Bo and Gari with Everett and Helen Dye, two faithful friends.

BELOW: The former Mercy Hospital building, centerpiece of a real estate deal God used to put Bo and Gari back on their feet financially. The building's single-word sign—MERCY— spoke volumes to Bo.

1001 MILWAUKEE STREET

Bo and Gari were glad to see their children flourish after struggling through their father's imprisonment.

BELOW: Ashley as "Miss Topeka" in the 1994 Miss Kansas pageant; Bo and Gari with Andy, who played football for the University of Colorado.

LEFT: Bo embraces his four grandchildren in 2014. CLOCKWISE: Bo; Kensie, 15; Brooke, 8; Katie, 11; Mitchell, 12.

I'd never experienced *literally* being in chains.

But I was about to.

One night in February—Tuesday the 4th—a guard told me, "Tomorrow morning you'll be picked up at 6:00 to go to the federal building."

I swallowed. "So what's this about?"

"I don't know."

Fear flooded through me. *It's happening*, I thought. There was some issue. More charges were going to be filed against me. The government was going to make my imprisonment permanent. My worst nightmare was coming true.

When I woke up early the next morning, my fears seemed to be confirmed. As if I were a serial killer, terrorist, or mental patient, I was shackled and chained. The cold steel links were heavy, making a chinking sound as the locks snapped shut.

It was hard to walk, and the muscles of my arms began to burn when I couldn't stretch. A prison van drove me to downtown Denver. I rode in silence.

Inside the federal court building, no one seemed able to tell me why I was there. I found myself taking an elevator to a holding tank in the basement.

I was there for hours, waiting. Still in chains.

I didn't feel like Samson, the biblical strongman wrapped in chains. I felt more like Jonah, trapped in the belly of the great fish. Or the New Testament's Paul and Silas, shackled in jail. But unlike them I wasn't singing, and no earthquake rumbled to my rescue.

Finally a deputy came to get me. Clinking and clanking, I trudged to the elevator and felt it rise.

Minutes later I stood in the office of the Deputy U.S. Attorney.

He looked the way he always had during the investigation, wearing his dark suit and tie, studious in his glasses. But he seemed surprised and flustered to see me shackled and chained.

A paper sack from Wendy's sat on his desk. "I . . . thought you might like to come in here . . . for a burger and a shake," he said.

And that was it.

There were no questions for me, no purpose for this meeting other than to say hello and have a hamburger. No doubt he had no idea I'd be shackled, chained, and held in the basement for hours. Whether out of guilt or some other motivation, he apparently was just trying to be kind.

Nice thought, I told myself. *Bad execution*.

I was relieved to know that the government wasn't ready to interrogate me or extend my incarceration, at least not yet. But it was a pretty awkward lunch.

It reminded me that the judicial system seemed to have no idea what the prison side was doing. It also made me think, *I guess God doesn't want me to miss any part of the federal prison system—including being shackled and chained.*

That night, I was sore but finally liberated from the bindings I'd worn for most of the day. *Glad it's over*, I wrote in my journal.

But of course it wasn't. God had other lessons for me, and school was just beginning.

Gray-Bar Hotel

I was so convinced that God wanted to correct my course, in fact, that I wrote a song about it. I'd loved playing and singing music since I was a teenager, and it seemed a natural thing to do.

The Lord had even provided accompaniment.

My first week at camp, I was exploring my new surroundings. In a closet at the end of an unfinished hallway I discovered an old and worn guitar. It was not quite full-sized but bigger than a toy, with steel strings that could still be tuned. No doubt it was worth less than $100, but it was priceless to me.

I was amazed to find it. The camp was like a sterile environment; everything allowed was accounted for, and everything else was contraband. The guards confiscated the latter and got rid of it.

Yet here was a guitar. It was as if God were saying, "I have a gift for you. It's here because I thought you might have some fun playing it."

So I did. Almost every day. It was comforting to entertain myself—and eventually other inmates. And the guards never tried to take it away.

One day an idea for a song came to me. I ended up calling it "The Gray-Bar Hotel," a term for prison that I picked up from the other guys. I even asked a young Native American inmate to work the phrase into a beaded belt that he made for me. I'd worn the belt for two or three days before the guards noticed it and said, "No, not funny. Contraband."

But they couldn't take away the song title—or the lyrics. The song went through at least two versions, but when I sang and played it for some of the other guys, I could tell they understood all too well what it meant. It went something like this:

When the judge looked down at me and said, "You're going,"
I knew that it was time to make a stand
I knew that it was time I started growing
Into everything it means to be a man.

So I kissed my wife and hugged my son and daughter
And tried to force just one more painful smile
I said, "You all be strong; I won't be gone too long
But they're takin' me away for a little while."

Chorus:
Now I'm stuck in the Gray-Bar Hotel
It's a little bit like livin' in hell
I stare out from the bars in my cold and lonely cell
I'm stuck in the Gray-Bar Hotel.

Well, that first night when they locked me down
I will not forget that sound

When that jailer turned that lock and key
I stared out to the prison guard and said,
"This life I choose is hard,
But it'll make a better man of me."

So I kissed my wife and hugged my son and daughter
And asked the Lord to heal and make me well
Prayed hard that I would learn every lesson
They teach here at the Gray-Bar Hotel.

Gari's Story

When Bo went to prison, it was during the high school basketball season. Andy found it tough not to have his number one fan in the stands. It was difficult for Bo to miss the games too. Our good friend Everett Dye went to all of them, taking copious notes on Andy's every move.

Andy also felt pressure to be "the man of the house" in Bo's absence. I tried hard to let him know he didn't need to do that.

I had no help on that front from one of Andy's coaches. When Andy told him what we were going through, the coach claimed Andy was the man of the house now. And the coach was going to do him a favor by being even harder on him than normal—because that would make him a man!

Angry, I confronted the coach. He said the same thing to me.

I told Andy we'd just have to live with it. But we didn't tell

Bo; he couldn't have done anything about it, and knowing would have caused him more pain.

Meanwhile, Ashley was a tremendous help at home—doing most of the chores I couldn't manage. It was also a joy to watch as dozens of prison visits and tons of cards and letters brought her closer to her dad.

I could see when we visited Bo that he desperately needed us. He lived for those times, drinking in our encouragement. The two days a week when he couldn't see us were especially difficult for him.

Sometimes visiting him was terrifying. He'd tell us what was happening in the camp, about guys he'd met. He didn't tell us all of it; we already couldn't bear having him there, and knowing the whole truth probably would have made it worse.

We prayed constantly for him. We prayed he would be smart as a fox, that God would give him wisdom and things to say and ways to survive. And for protection. We prayed for that all the time, still fearing he would be raped, or worse. As Bo said, we truly felt threatened from all sides.

I was also concerned about finances.

Fortunately, Phil Anschutz kept his promise to keep paying us and to hold the job open for Bo. I was so thankful for Phil—and so upset with others who chose to disassociate from Bo, thereby causing us to lose income we'd been counting on.

But then I realized the Lord had freed Bo from other sources of stress by having these tough financial things happen. I became grateful, which helped keep my resentment in check. When I was tempted to make some angry calls, I thought, *No—I need to make my way through this entire time in such a way that the Lord is pleased with me, so that when I look back I have no regrets.*

But I knew how precarious our financial situation was.

I kept telling Ashley and Andy that God was in control and we'd be okay. I wasn't just saying that to reassure them. I believed it. I could see it every day when Bo faced danger and the Lord answered our prayers for protection, and when friends helped us financially.

And I could see it as He began to use prison to free Bo from the spiritual and emotional chains that had bound him for so long.

CHAPTER 9

RIDING THE PINE

"The Gray-Bar Hotel" was about to become my theme song. The longer I was in prison, the clearer it was that I had much to learn.

I was doing what athletes in almost every sport referred to as "riding the pine." It meant sitting on the bench, out of the action. As an athlete I'd ridden the pine before—sometimes due to an injury, sometimes because another player was doing a better job, sometimes for mouthing off to a coach.

Riding the pine had never been fun. But I learned a few things as a result.

Now I had the feeling that, if I paid attention, I was about to do the same thing in prison. For the first time in my life I was completely on the sidelines, doing pine time because of the mess I helped create.

I began to believe that if I hadn't been sentenced to prison I would have missed everything God had for me. Apparently, nothing short of federal prison would have kept me from being the guy who was going to do everything, do it his way, and under his own power—the kid who was determined to earn acceptance by scoring 20 points every time there was a game.

The learning process was already underway. I was about to gain insights from many teachers, but five of them would play special roles in my pine-time curriculum.

Pride 101

One of those teachers was Jim Dobson.

On March 8, 1992—the tenth anniversary of the day Cherry Hills Community Church opened its doors—I was sitting behind bars. Suddenly I realized, *You won't be standing with the other founders of the church being recognized for the church's success. In fact, you can't even attend the event. You're not going anywhere.*

Feeling sorry for myself, I turned on my little radio and started listening to Jim's *Focus on the Family* broadcast. He was talking about how proud he'd always been of getting his name on a major tennis trophy at the University of Southern California.

About 15 years later he'd had a rude awakening. A friend

of his visited the campus and found something lying in an outdoor garbage can. It was the trophy, long forgotten by everyone else and headed for the landfill.

The discovery gave Dr. Dobson a reality check: *If you live long enough, life will trash your trophies.* Most of our accomplishments, he realized, aren't quite as accomplished or eternal as we think they are.

It sounded like my experience. Here I was, having thought for a decade that I was so vital to the founding of that church. Now I saw that, even though it was a significant event that gave me much joy and satisfaction, the church would do fine celebrating without me.

Another trophy trashed.

God's message to me seemed clear: *I could've used anybody to start that church.*

It wasn't a feel-good message, but it was the truth. Jim Dobson didn't know it, but he'd just given me a new perspective on one of my old problems—pride.

Success Suit

In prison, there was plenty of time to read—and to be God's student.

That's how I was able to study a book called *Sidetracked in the Wilderness* by Michael Wells—five times. Michael was another professor in my Camp Englewood course.

If there was anyone who felt sidetracked in the wilderness, it was me. I immersed myself in that paperback, underlining passages and writing notes in the margins. So much of what the author said seemed aimed right between my eyes.

He talked about "Grade A idols," dangerous because they were respectable. Even ministry could be an idol, he said. He gave an example: "A wife tells a man that he's failing at home as a father and husband, so he withdraws to the Church where people will tell him what a wonderful job he does."[4]

That sounded an awful lot like me, so I underlined the passage.

I did the same when I read a passage about how, when we feel unacceptable to God, we often end up looking in all the wrong places for affirmation and love. I'd looked for those things in achievement—no matter the cost. As Michael put it, "Man becomes thoroughly and intensely self-centered in his quest."[5]

I wrote in the margin: *Me! 3/16/92 in prison, #1 lesson!*

Later I wrote another comment on a scrap of paper and stuck it between pages 76 and 77: *Love and acceptance— everyone's hero!* Yeah, I'd tried to be everybody's hero. How had that worked out?

Then came this nugget:

If we could regain rationality, we would conclude that the self-centered life is comprised of emptiness, weariness, and misery, with the blind leading the blind. Unfortunately, self-life is a force much greater than reason, capable of enslaving mankind.[6]

I underlined it and wrote in the margin, *Me in prison, long before prison.* I'd been enslaved, all right—for more years than I could remember.

A few pages later, the author had me pegged:

It becomes evident that no one will accept or love us. . . . Therefore, to milk love and acceptance out of others, we run to an imaginary sewing machine to make a "success suit."[7]

I'd tried so hard to earn acceptance—from my dad, from other people, from God. Now my "success suit" had been replaced with a lopsided pair of prison pants. I underlined the insight and wrote in the margin: *Me!*

The next section that hit me like a line drive was kind of funny—but painful:

Suppose I could persuade you that you are a rabbit! How long could you hop? Five, ten minutes, maybe fifteen? After you had hopped so long, what would you be ready to do? Stand up, of course! Your whole body would begin to ache from jumping and pretending to be what you are not. When you are living in your success suit, you are merely hopping. You feel you must, of course, for who would accept the real you? So you get up at 7:00 a.m., put on your success suit, and begin to hop! By 6:00 p.m. what are you ready to do? Stand up, rip off that uncomfortable suit that has been suffocating you, and be what you really are! Therefore, the world has the benefit of knowing you in your success suit while you hop, but your family reaps the consequences of knowing the real you.[8]

Ouch. Had Michael Wells been watching a videotape of my life? After underlining the words, I dog-eared the corner of the page for good measure. In the margin I wrote: *I've been hopping for 20 years!*

Fortunately, the author soon hinted at a solution: replacing our old identity with a new one. Then daily events wouldn't run our lives, and we could leave behind the burden of coping with our idols. I wasn't sure yet what that meant, but it sounded good.

I underlined that section and wrote in the margin: *Daily help—new life!*

As I sat reading in my prison schoolhouse, another passage hit close to home:

This book is for the defeated. . . . *The true depth of a person's faith is revealed in his ability to accept forgiveness in the midst of his deepest defeat.* . . . When you have done nothing wrong, perhaps the thought of death does not frighten you because you are carrying with you a nice little bag of good works with which you think the Lord will be pleased. However, failure reveals where you have really put your trust; if in its midst you shrink back in fear, you prove that your righteousness was based on what you could do and not on what He has done. Many in the midst of failure refuse forgiveness, continuing a self-inflicted punishment until they believe they have paid the price.[9]

I underlined that paragraph, then wrote in the margin: *3/20/92—This is how I feel in prison!*

Later I stuck another scrap of paper between the pages with this note: *3/29/92—This is how I feel in prison, "cut off," "benched."*

I didn't want to stay there. Reading on, I discovered Michael's Bible-based plan for getting off the pine.

It began with repentance and pressing on. God wants us to come to Him in weakness and humility, not the fake strength of what we thought we could achieve. The Lord isn't prodding us to do great things, but to be faithful in the small ones—like forgiving, loving unlovable people, and storing up treasures in heaven instead of on earth. God wants to replace our old selves with the life of His Son.

Slapping patches on our weaknesses or transforming ourselves with our willpower or our works isn't the answer. The answer is to exchange our lives for Christ's, as Paul said in Galatians 2:20:

I have been crucified with Christ and I no longer live, but Christ lives in me. The life I live in the

body, I live by faith in the Son of God, who loved
me and gave himself for me.

I kept writing in the margins:

*Work = an expression of faith, not trying to
produce faith.*

This is why I'm here—3/20/92.

Great stuff! God did it! On my way back up!

At least I hoped I was.

For the moment, I had a lot to think about. It was excit-
ing, overwhelming—and a little scary.

I wrote in my journal,

*I sobbed for a long time today. I've been broken,
big time, and I feel like this is just where God wants
me to be. I'm crushed. I started reading* Sidetracked
in the Wilderness *today and got a lot of peace
from it. Then I called home and Gari was sobbing
too. I need to see myself as God's student and not as
a victim.*

Michael Wells was quite a teacher, all right. But was I willing
to learn—no matter how uncomfortable it might become?

Staying in Line

Mr. Wells wasn't the only author I turned to in prison. Another was Gary Smalley.

I'd known Gary for several years after meeting him through Jim and Shirley Dobson.

As I served my sentence, I read Gary's book *Joy That Lasts*—twice. It was all about recharging your batteries and refilling your fuel tank—just right for a guy who'd been running on empty for as long as he could remember.

Gary explained that in life we can become so involved with and drained by our problems, and projects, and people, and hobbies, and on and on, that—just like a car—we run out of gas and find ourselves empty. What we need to do is periodically find time and ways to refuel and recharge our lives so that doesn't happen.

Now I realized, *That's what prison is doing for me. Slowing me down. Making me stop. Making me regroup.*

The question was, how was I supposed to fill that tank and charge those batteries?

Between Gary's insights and my notes in the margins, we practically had a conversation on the subject.

It started with the title of his first chapter: "Reaching Bottom Is the First Step Up."[10] I'd certainly managed to do that.

After observing that every crisis can be a step toward a better life, Gary recalled a difficult situation he'd faced— a conflict with another leader. That sounded familiar too.

Gary had responded by praying that God would help him not to expect anyone other than the Lord to fill his life.

God's Spirit alone, I wrote in the margin.

Gary also prayed for healthy relationships with his wife and kids, and for wisdom to be the best husband and father he could. Finally he asked for a friend to help him learn more, resolve his turmoil over the conflict, and obey God more fully.

I wrote in the margin again: *I need this*.

When things didn't go exactly as he'd hoped, Gary told God that instead of trying to fix things himself, he'd let the Lord prove His faithfulness by relying on Him.

In the margin I wrote, *4/24/92—My spirit was weakening this morning. Two miles on the track, ½ hour. Miserably pitiful—[thought my being in prison wasn't] fair. Then came here and read this book! Let God prove His faithfulness in your life!*

For Gary Smalley, that had been a major turning point. Soon he saw that he could trust God, even when he didn't understand what the Lord was doing. His confidence in God grew, and he started praying about other things too.

My marginal comment: *In prison! Relax and trust Him too!! Even when I don't understand what He's doing!*

Gary admitted having doubted that he'd ever get any answers from God or be allowed to serve Him again.

This is how I feel! I wrote at the edge of the page.

Gary came to see that if he'd never gone through that hard time, he wouldn't have known how faithful God was or how deep their relationship could be.

This is what prison has done for me! I responded in the margin. *I'll get out and be out if I'll listen to Him.*

"Imagine an unrighteous, wicked judge . . . ," Gary wrote.[11]

That didn't take too much imagination. I drew a star by that one.

Gary confessed how, even after he'd moved away from the man with whom he'd been in conflict, Gary still resented him. He knew that was wrong, but couldn't seem to shake his feelings of betrayal and desire for revenge.

Every day for two years, Gary prayed when he went jogging, "Lord, I'm in line again, along with many of Your children. I must admit how upset I still am with [that man]. I don't know how You're going to do it, but I know You're going to free me. Maybe this is the day! And if not today, perhaps tomorrow!"[12]

Gary recorded, "After two years of getting in line every day and requesting that freedom, it finally came."[13]

Free of resentment! I wrote on the page. *Lord, free me, too! Thanks, Gary!*

Gary explained that any Christian could know the joy of trusting God. But none of us could take pride in what he did because it was only possible through God's faithfulness, not our spirituality.

His faithfulness, not my spirituality! I echoed in the margin.

Gary acknowledged that it was only when he depended completely on Christ that he was where the Lord wanted him.

Me, too, I wrote. That described my current position in the Gray-Bar Hotel.

"Unfortunately," Gary added, "many today never claim God's promised packages. We leave His gifts in the warehouse of heaven, either because we never ask or because we get out of line too soon."[14]

I underlined that one. *Don't get out of line too soon*, I wrote in the margin. *Keep praying . . . perseverance.*

I began to see what I'd missed before prison, going too fast and running on fumes. I had nothing left to offer anybody, especially my family. I'd be doing all of us a favor by refilling my tank and charging my batteries. I'd have to be more intentional about that in the future—assuming I had one.

One day I received a greeting card—a fold-out one that said on the cover, "I used to feel like a helpless caterpillar, bruised from the pain of life."

Inside it said, "But I've finally been wrapped by the Lord's healing cocoon of love. I can already tell that the wings of a butterfly are beginning to emerge. Soon I'll be healed and more beautiful than ever. I can't wait! Thanks to You, Lord, my life has taken on new meaning."

It was from Gary Smalley.

His handwritten message said,

Bo,

. . . I've thought of you many times and continue to pray for His grace to bless you and help you see little by little how all this will work out for His glory and your rich benefit!! I spent five hours this week with

Ollie North and he says there are great things ahead for you!

When you can, each "Thank You, Lord, for this mess" response is like a single strand of silk wrapped around us. Soon He will allow us to fly anew with much more brilliant colors!

We all love you—He is all we need anyway!

Gary Smalley

P.S. I tried to visit you and was blocked.

I was sorry I'd missed Gary's visit. But I was glad that, thanks to his book, we'd had an important conversation anyway.

Why I Did It

God also used a fourth "wise man" while I was in prison to teach me a thing or two.

He was Bobb Biehl, an old friend of our family. Toward the end of March he called Gari and asked whether he could be my only visitor that day. He was writing a book called *Why You Do What You Do* and wanted to ask me some questions.

We ended up spending much of the day together. We talked about many things, especially how my past had influenced my present.

"What you were doing on the playground in the fourth grade is probably what you're doing as an adult," Bobb said. I remembered what I'd been like in fourth grade, standing up for my polio-stricken friend, Hank, on the playground.

I also recalled how bossy I'd been when I did it, ordering the other kids around because I thought I knew best.

Sure enough, that was pretty much how I'd acted before going to prison—trying to help people, but often going about it like a bull in a china shop.

"That fits me 100 percent," I told Bobb, confirming his theory.

Bobb also seemed to understand my desire to be everybody's hero. Many other adult children of alcoholics felt the same way. If our fathers had too much to drink in a restaurant and said something rude to a waitress, we were supposed to rescue them by going in the kitchen and apologizing: "Dad's a great guy; he didn't mean to hurt your feelings."

People like me had started doing things like that when we were 10 years old, and some of us had done it for the rest of our lives. We were the heroes, trying to rescue others just as we'd covered for a parent's bad behavior. It was a hard habit to break.

Bobb helped me understand why I was in prison.

Rebuilding

Shortly after Bobb's visit, Gari sent me a card. It said in part:

I can't believe how you've handled a situation that is designed to destroy your manhood, your self-respect, your belief in who you are . . . and is constantly telling you [that] you are a failure. But you are not

a failure—you are in God's design for your life.
He knew before you were born, and these days were
ordained for you.

Gari was a wonderful wife. But she was more. She was the fifth teacher on my federal prison faculty.

Her cards and letters were so gracious, so forgiving. And there was plenty to forgive.

I knew Gari had paid a price for marrying me—and not just since I'd gone to prison. My insensitivity toward her had displayed itself more times than I wanted to recall.

Unfortunately, I could remember some of them clearly.

Three times during the first few years of our marriage we'd found ourselves at parties, at odds over a thoughtless remark I'd made. She'd tear up and say, "You just said something to me that really hurt me. So now tell me something you love about me, or we're going home."

I'd think, *I don't know why I'm so stupid. I can't get this straight. I didn't mean to hurt you. Let me think about this, because I want to stay at the party. And I don't want you crying.*

Things hadn't improved when I'd thrown myself 200 percent into business and ministry. Gari had tried to tell me how neglected she'd felt, but I'd never really understood.

Now I was beginning to.

Despite my being away from home, it sometimes felt as if there were fewer communication barriers now than there had been before. When Gari visited, we had hours face-to-face to discuss any and all topics. When we wrote letters, we could say things—positive and negative—that seemed harder to say in person. After one particularly painful discussion in the visitation room, I wrote Gari this letter:

> *Our Sunday night visit was super! I really appreciate your being so honest with me. Even though it hurt some, it mainly felt great because I'm trying to work through all the trash in my life while I'm here. All I can tell you is, no one has meant as much to me— or means as much to me—as you do. I must have just fallen into a sleepy type of funk to treat you with such cruelty. I thank you for forgiving me. Through my period of misconduct you have been 100 percent supportive of me. Never a cruel word—not one— and I'll never forget it. I love you more every day and I can't wait to have the chance to show you that I'm changing. . . .*

Even when tough issues arose in our talks, Gari always seemed hopeful about the future of our marriage. One day I opened a letter from her that said:

> *I am excited for how much all four of us are growing, even though at the bottom of all our hearts is a layer of sadness and grief that is exhausting in ways we don't even know.*
>
> *But as you said, when we are together again, our appreciation of each other—our love, our blessings in*

being a family, our marriage—will never be taken
for granted. . . .

Frankly, we've rarely spent time lately truly
conversing as we do now while you are in prison—
everyone has been so busy, but now it's all we have,
and it is time I am very grateful for.

Both of us seemed to know that our marriage wouldn't be
better in the future if we didn't start changing things in the
present. Gari's words in this letter reminded me that we had
work to do:

I hope we can stop criticizing each other and ourselves,
and recognize that we are all human and make
mistakes. . . . Instead, let's build each other in love and
concentrate and comment on and believe in our God-
given strengths. The parts of us that God has allowed us
to have that are the very best.

Life is tough enough. There is always someone waiting
to shoot you down. We don't need to shoot ourselves. Let's
live more, love more, laugh more, turn our heads when
others do us wrong, and barely see the faults in others.
Let's see the miracle of Christ in each person's uniqueness.
And let's enjoy it—especially in each other.

In a way, prison was giving us a second chance to rebuild our
marriage. It might even help make me a better husband—if
I could learn what God wanted to teach me with Gari's help.

There was far too much going on in our relationship for me to record in my little burgundy journal. But one night I gave it a shot:

> *I walked for 2.5 hours today and prayed the whole time with Carl and prayed for all the inmates here at the camp. Gari and I had a great talk today. She said I don't talk to her enough; she almost enjoys the fact that now I'm in prison and our visits are so long. I love her honesty. She is Superwoman.*

And quite an instructor, I might add.

Gari's Story

Sometimes during visitation we'd watch inmates sitting around, not spending one minute trying to figure out why they were there. We'd hear them saying, "I need to get an appeal," and "That so-and-so—if he hadn't done that, this wouldn't have happened to me."

They never seemed to ask God, "Why am I here? What is there about me that You want to change? What do You want to free me from?"

That wasn't the case with Bo. He was totally humbled and seeking God. He was beginning to realize he'd had chains wrapped around him long before he went to prison—most of them dating back to his childhood. He was chained by being driven to win, to be the hero. Even his enthusiasm for life and love for helping people succeed had brought him trouble at times. Now it looked as if living behind the bars of a real, tangible federal prison would be the mechanism the Lord might use to free him.

I remembered the friend who'd called the day before Bo's sentencing to predict that when the judge opened his mouth, Bo would be hearing God's grace. Who knew something as severe as prison could be that grace?

Bobb Biehl's visit with Bo was a great help. It showed us how many of Bo's chains had been forged over the years, giving us clues about how they might be broken.

Coming from homes where alcohol was a problem hadn't affected Bo and me in exactly the same ways. I looked for safety and control through my perfectionism and people-pleasing. He became the guy who tried to fix everything, make everyone happy, and solve everyone's problems—often at his expense and sometimes our family's.

God's grace in prison also extended to our marriage. Both of us knew we had a good marriage, but like most couples, we wanted it to be great. We'd known and taught that being each other's number one priority (after the Lord) was God's design. But we'd both slipped on each other's list. We'd been trying to survive my illness and make things as good as we could for our children, and our relationship had taken a back seat. Neither of us had the energy for more. Bo was stressed in so many ways—keeping our lives going, keeping me going.

The added stress of prison changed all that. We needed

each other so much now and could only find true solace in our love. We tackled the tough issues in our marriage during that time, the ones we'd let stack up. The pressure cooker of prison and my illness gave us the courage to truly look at our lives and improve.

I had learned that 90 percent of couples divorce when one spouse has a major illness like mine. And 80 percent of couples divorce when one spouse goes to prison. Our marriage only *improved*—a miracle showing God's loving power in our lives.

Bo was changing in many ways. For one, "riding the pine" was giving him time to truly look at his temper and why his anger had exploded at times. He'd rarely aimed that temper at me, knowing criticism would crater me for a month and he'd have to pick up the pieces.

God was helping me *feel* the unconditional love Bo truly had for me. I was becoming far more balanced and secure in every aspect of my life. Thanks to my treatment at the Minirth Meier Clinic as well as the sifting we were going through, I wasn't quite the people-pleaser or rescuer I'd been.

I was feeling God's unconditional love in my life, and only rarely becoming afraid. I was less of a perfectionist— even though, like most people, I'd sometimes revert to old patterns when things became uncomfortable.

So, out of our pain—my illness, Bo's imprisonment, our childhoods surrounded by alcohol abuse—we grew together, not apart. It was an amazing thing.

CHAPTER 10

HOPE IN SIGHT

IN HER LETTERS AND VISITS, Gari was a great motivator. She was, after all, the one who'd written to me, "If you allow prison to keep you from being all that God meant you to be, then Satan has won!"

She wasn't the only person who assured me that my pine time wasn't permanent. Dan Stavely—a football coach, friend, and my former mentor at the University of Colorado who signed himself "The Old Coach" wrote me this:

There are a lot of folks in the Good Book who stubbed their toes and yet came back and played a great hand for the Lord. David, a man after God's own heart, is an

*example. God can and does recycle folks and uses them
in a wonderful way. Keep your chin up and remember
where you are—in a fertile field of evangelism. God
may have sent you in there because there is some hard-
nosed young chap who could never open the door to his
heart except you have that special gift that would enable
you to get the job done.*

Coach Stavely wasn't the only one who encouraged me to
see prison as a mission field and to see myself as a harvester.
But I couldn't see myself as an apostle Paul. Paul had been
imprisoned for preaching the gospel, not for bank fraud.

There was a reason I'd resigned all those ministry positions. I was here to learn, not teach.

Still, I began to find myself faced with opportunities to
do what the coach and others were encouraging. The need
was great; I couldn't just turn away.

One such opportunity came because of the prison's mail-
call routine. One of the guards would gather the inmates,
who would stand around, waiting. The guard would then go
to the front of the group and hand out one letter at a time,
calling the last name of each recipient, who would come up
and get his letter.

The guards never sorted the mail. They'd just bundle it all
up and read out the names on the letters, one at a time, in no
particular order: "Jones . . . Smith . . . Wilson . . . Smith . . .
Jones . . ."

It wasn't like they stacked it together, put a rubber band

around it, and said "Mitchell" and handed you your letters. That was why the whole thing took so long.

For months mail call had become an increasingly uncomfortable experience. Most days the guard would hand me half a dozen letters or more. One day I counted 27. Many inmates received no letters at all. For them, mail call meant disappointment and discouragement.

Most of the men would stand there when the process got underway, excited, anxious. I could tell they were thinking, *Did I get a letter today?*

When they didn't, and I had my name called 27 times, it was pretty awkward. I thought, *Okay, it might feel better to everybody if I wasn't here.* I was thankful for every letter sent to me, but it was hard to face the others and feel so bad for them.

After one such day in April, having received a stack of mail, I returned to my room and found one of my roommates in tears. Blaine said, "I've been here seven months. I haven't gotten as many letters in that whole time as you've gotten most days. What am I doing wrong?"

I could almost feel his loneliness. Like so many guys here, he probably hadn't planted many seeds of love in other people's hearts before ending up in prison. It was no wonder so many inmates received so few letters.

I explained to Blaine that a family of faith was available to him if he received Christ and built relationships with Christian brothers and sisters. "It's about Christian friends and family," I said. "You need Christ."

To my surprise, Blaine was so open to what I was saying that he prayed to receive Christ—right there, that day.

His journey was underway. I saw changes in him over the next month because of his new faith. He was released from prison before he started receiving much mail—but I was certain that his life outside would be filled with the love and joy he'd been missing every day.

Well, I thought, *there's one good thing that came out of mail call—and all the letters my family and friends have been writing.*

Then there was Grady.

Grady was an older African-American man, very short, with a big smile—and few teeth. He minded his own business, and everybody liked him.

Grady had been attending the Prison Fellowship Bible study for about a month. One night, after the meeting was over, I could tell he just hadn't been tracking with the discussion.

When everyone had left, I asked him in the hallway, "Grady, do you have a clue what we're talking about in here?"

"Not a clue," he said.

"Why do you continue to come?"

"It makes me feel good," he answered.

I said, "Would you like to know *why* it makes you feel good?"

"Yes."

He and I sat down for about half an hour. I told him the same thing Don Reeverts had told me decades before—how to have a personal relationship with Christ.

Finally I asked, "Would you like to pray this prayer with me and become a Christian?"

"Yes," he said. And he did.

Then I asked, "Do you understand now what we just did together?"

He nodded.

As I walked to my room at the other end of the building, a couple of Grady's friends came up to me. They looked worried. "What have you done to Grady?" they demanded.

"What do you mean?"

One of them declared, "He tells us now there's *two* Gradys!"

I knew then that he *did* understand. There was a physical Grady and a spiritual one. The spiritual one had been born again that night.

"Well, there *are* two Gradys," I said. "If you want to hear the whole story, you'll have to sit down sometime and I'll tell you about it."

After they left, I wondered how this all fit into God's plan. Did I have to go to prison so Grady could hear the gospel?

Half-joking, I asked the Lord, *I had to come all the way out here for this? Couldn't we have met somewhere on a weekend retreat?*

I could tell the answer was no. Our worlds had intersected only because of prison.

On April 19 another ministry opportunity presented itself. It was Easter Sunday.

Since resigning as associate pastor of our church, I'd avoided pulpits, platforms, and preaching. But the inmates were having a morning Easter service, and I was asked to speak.

I said yes. I went around inviting some of the meanest guys in Camp Englewood—and they showed up.

So did my friends Martha Dell and Jerry, both successful Denver businesspeople in their mid-60s. I could see Martha Dell's familiar curly hair and glasses as I spoke, but she wasn't her usual upbeat self. She cried through the whole service, heartbroken to see what I was going through.

But the service was just the beginning of that special Easter Sunday. Former Denver Seminary President Vernon Grounds visited me for two hours, full of encouragement. Then Chuck Colson, the legendary, born-again Nixon "hatchet man" and founder of Prison Fellowship, spent the afternoon with us, as did former Senator Bill Armstrong and a whole group of people. The finale was a chapel with chaplain Del.

When the day was over, I dared to think that I might really have a future after all. Could it be that I wouldn't be riding the pine forever?

That night I summed it up in my journal:

My best Easter EVER was today here in prison.

One more opportunity to minister arose—though at first it looked like a threat.

It came the morning Julie from the Cold Room left a

message with my roommate Zack: I was to be at her office by noon. She didn't say why.

I panicked, convinced that something had gone wrong. Maybe an inmate had accused me of breaking a rule. Maybe the government had found something else to charge me with. Maybe some guards had figured out a way to get back at me for my remarks to the federal judges.

I sat down with pen and paper and made a list of 16 things I thought Julie might want to see me about. I prayed that God would calm my spirit.

When I stepped into her office, Mr. Swanson was there. That didn't make me less nervous.

"We're familiar with your file," Julie told me. "We know you're an ordained minister."

She told me about an inmate named Peter. He was young, a Native American, a soft-spoken family man, and a drug offender.

Julie didn't know it, but I'd already met Peter—in the weight room, two months before. I'd asked him, "Why are you in here?"

"Drugs," he said.

"At least you're done with that terrible part of your life."

"No, I'm not done at all," he replied. "I'll still do drugs."

"Why?"

"It makes me feel great," he said.

"I've got something that will make you feel even better than that," I volunteered.

"What?"

"Jesus Christ."

That hadn't exactly piqued his interest. Still, when I'd asked him to do me a favor, he'd obliged. He was the guy who'd made me a beaded belt that included the phrase "Welcome to the Gray-Bar Hotel" in its design.

Now Julie was asking me to do Peter a favor. "Would you share Christ with him before you leave? Peter has AIDS, and he's dying."

I was stunned. After a pause I asked, "Do Peter's roommates know he has AIDS?"

"No."

I said, "I think maybe you should let them know, since we live in such close quarters."

They didn't promise anything, but asked me to let them know whether I'd talk to Peter.

Not knowing how to approach him, I thought about it for half a day. Finally I decided that asking where he was with Christ was the least I could do.

As I walked up to Peter, I felt God was again giving me the words to say.

"Peter," I began, "you and I share something in common."

"What's that?" he asked.

"I've been told I have a terminal illness," I replied.

His expression turned serious. "How long do you have to live?"

"They haven't been able to narrow it down. Something between five days and 50 years."

He smiled, a big smile. Then he paused.

"We're all dying, aren't we?" he asked.

"Yes, we are. And there are things we need to consider while we're still alive that will determine the direction we go after death."

I asked him whether he'd thought about Jesus Christ and who He claimed to be.

"No," he said.

So we talked it through, much as I had with Blaine and Grady: Here's the Good News, here's the choice you have to make. Yes to Christ, or no.

"Have you made that choice?" I asked.

"No," Peter said.

"Would you like to?"

"Yes."

And he prayed—right there, right then—as he chose to believe in Christ.

I was unable to track what happened to Peter—in terms of his health.

I believe I know, though, what ultimately happened to him. He met the Savior he'd received that day. I was grateful that God let me be part of it.

Waiting for a Move

Knowing that God could use me right there in prison was like a light at the end of a tunnel, but its flicker was faint. Would I be useful to God outside of the Gray-Bar Hotel? I knew I still had a lot of pine time to do before that could happen.

There was another light of hope glimmering in the distance, though, and it seemed closer. At least my family, friends, and I had been praying that it was.

There was a chance that, at some point, I'd be able to move from Camp Englewood to a halfway house. I'd still be under the thumb of the prison system, but I'd be able to work during the day—and, more important, make scheduled visits home to be with my family.

It was a goal of many, if not all, inmates. They talked constantly about getting early releases to halfway houses, home arrest, and furloughs. But thinking and talking about such things was mostly a waste of time.

Here's how it worked: When the Bureau of Prisons decided you'd had enough of the harsher punishment, the order would come from somewhere that you'd been reassigned to a halfway house. The date of transfer was called your "out date"—the day you were scheduled to get out.

We tried not to get our hopes up, knowing how badly things could go when you were in the system. And there was a chance that, even if an out date was scheduled, things could go wrong.

This was my mind-set on April 15, at 3:40 p.m., when I was called into Mr. Swanson's office.

He told me that my out date was May 22. I would be entering the next phase of my imprisonment—and my time on the spiritual bench.

At least that was the plan.

Word got around quickly. Before I could even make it back to my room, everybody else in the camp seemed to know about it. It turned out that only a few guys were actually happy for a prisoner with an out date. Most were angry because they were still stuck behind bars. There was a constant threat that someone might attack you in your sleep with a "blanket party."

I didn't know anyone who'd had it happen to him. But the mental picture of three guys covering you in a blanket while you were asleep and beating you unconscious was enough to keep me alert—not that I was sleeping much anyway.

A more common problem for prisoners assigned an out date was being intimidated by inmates who wanted your possessions—your sweatpants, radio, shoes, and maybe a book or two.

That happened to me when the biggest guy in camp cornered me in my room one afternoon.

His nickname was Flakey. A kid in a big man's body, he was aggressive and loud, playful but dangerous.

"Hey, man," he growled at me. "We don't think you're spending enough time hanging out with us black guys!"

Once more the Lord seemed to help me with a response. "Flake," I said, "who do you think I hang around with the most?"

His head lowered a little and his voice grew quiet. "God," he answered.

"So, if you were me, would you rather spend your time hanging around with God or with you?"

"God," he said softly.

"Alright," I said. "We agree on that. So why don't you just tell me what you'd like me to give you before I leave?"

He told me he'd like my radio if it wasn't already promised to someone.

I was more than happy to give it to him.

It was much easier, I explained, just to ask a friend for something than it was to try to bully it out of him.

Sensing that he'd heard enough lecturing from me for one day, I backed off. I reminded him, "My inmate number's been etched into that radio, so you could get in trouble. But it'll be your problem, not mine, because I'm leaving. But the day I leave, you can have it."

At least I hoped I was leaving. So did my family. They'd heard about the hostility against inmates who'd received their out dates. Andy was especially nervous for me. He sounded glad to hear my voice on the phone each morning and my report that no one had attacked me during the night.

From the day I was assigned my out date, our family rode an emotional roller coaster that was reflected in my journal:

APRIL 15: *[I was told] today that I would be released to a halfway house on May 22. Today is Andy's birthday, and this will be my birthday present to him. I can't wait to tell Andy tomorrow night, and Ashley and Gari, too!*

APRIL 16: *I told my family about the May 22 date and everyone was very excited.*

APRIL 23: *Whole camp had a random urine analysis today. It's a little weird and a little scary. One month* *to go and I'm out of here. I feel ready to leave. Ashley is feeling better. Today was the first day I allowed myself to reflect on how hard this has been, and I thought of what it must have been like for Gari to sit on our bed at home and write my name in T-shirts and underwear while she prepared to pack me for prison. What a mess I've created! I woke up [feeling] down today, thinking these thoughts.*

APRIL 27: *Great visit tonight. Ashley and Andy prayed over me. We were all very happy.*

MAY 5: *Ashley very sick today. Threw up all night. Scares me a lot. Feel funny today because I'm close to my out date. Can't wait to see my family Thursday.*

MAY 7: *Praise the Lord. I started pre-release class today. Also, my friend Jake Edson came out for a great visit. Two more weeks if all goes well. I'm still anxious. Please forgive me, God. Gari really ministered to me today, and I needed it so much.*

MAY 15: *This is my last full week. I woke up anxious and fearful. Please forgive me, God, and help me to trust You. I got a firm time, 9:00 a.m., that I'll be leaving prison on May 22. It feels great. I had to sign papers and get fingerprinted and have my picture taken again. I told my friends at prison camp about it. Some were excited and some were jealous.*

Out Date

The night before I was scheduled to leave prison, May 21, my roommates and I gathered to pray.

I prayed, "Lord, if I haven't learned every lesson You have for me to learn through this process, I pray that all the paperwork would blow up and that I would stay here until I learn every lesson."

It wasn't just a remote possibility. In fact, it was common for something to be messed up with these release dates. If that happened, it could be as long as three more weeks before your out date really meant *out*.

My roommates all protested my prayer, saying things like, "Whoa, whoa! Stop! Don't pray that here! Pray that tomorrow night! Get to the halfway house!"

But I didn't retract what I'd said. Despite all my fear that something would go wrong, I didn't want this experience to be in vain. *I'm glad to have this date*, I thought. *But I'm only glad if I've learned what God had for me to learn.*

I packed my belongings, which didn't take much time. Everything I had fit in one small box.

Looking down at that box, I said, "Wait a minute, guys. Everybody over here for a second."

I said, "Now, I have missed my family desperately, and my friends. But other than that I really haven't missed anything—and my whole life is in this one tiny little box!"

We had a good chuckle about it. They knew exactly what I meant. It was amazing how simple life could be when all the extras were stripped away. Prison tended to relieve you of all the things that weren't necessary—including, I hoped, some parts of myself that needed to be left behind.

I knew I'd miss all these guys, especially my good friend Marv Morrison. Later he sent me a description he'd written of the time we'd spent together:

> *I had been an inmate at Camp Englewood for about six months when Bo first arrived. I first saw him walking around the exercise track the evening he arrived, looking about how I must have looked the first day I arrived— depressed, fearful, and wondering what God might have in store for me and my family now. I went out to talk to him, and in a few minutes knew this was a Christian brother I wanted to get to know better.*
>
> *He had been assigned to another room (we lived in four-man rooms, sometimes with five or six men in them), but we were able to get him moved into the room I was in. Bo changed the whole atmosphere in our room. Bo did many things to encourage, uplift, and entertain us. Somehow he [found a guitar] to entertain us and even composed a few songs to fit our situation. Sometimes it felt more like a Young Life camp than a prison room.*
>
> *It didn't take Bo long to realize that he was where he was for a purpose. . . . I remember once we were in the workout room and Bo said to an inmate something like, "You are working on your body on the outside; how are you on the inside?" Tears came to the inmate's eyes, and*

Bo shared the gospel with him. Bo has a way of reaching many.

As I look back, I can see the many ways that God was caring for me during this time of trial. Putting Bo in my life was a big one.

The morning of my out date finally arrived, and later I wrote this in my journal:

MAY 22: *I woke up this morning at 4:30 a.m. totally excited, hoping that nothing would go wrong and trusting God. We prayed again in our room. Christ is number one in my life and I love Him and His Word more than ever. Hap was there to say good-bye. Zack took me to the jail at 7:45 a.m. Carl and Marv Morrison rode over with us. We hugged each other for a long time and said good-bye. At 8:45 my family came to pick me up. Andy brought me a Subway sandwich and Ashley brought me two cinnamon rolls. We all drove to the halfway house to fill out the papers there. I met my new roommate, who is a strong Christian and often gives his testimony at Prison Fellowship conferences. Another miracle. Then got to go home for a two-hour visit, my first in a long, long time. It felt great.*

It was the last entry I would write in my little fake-leather journal.

But it was definitely not the end of the story.

Gari's Story

On Easter, when Bo spoke in the service and all those friends came to visit him, I was too sick to be there. But I was glad that Bo seemed to be dipping his toe in ministry again.

In prison, he'd been reluctant to get anywhere near a leadership role. When I'd told him about Charlie's Philippians 1:13 vision, for instance, Bo didn't seem to want to hear it at first. He thought it made him "look special" with the Lord and didn't think he deserved any encouragement.

He was so broken. All he wanted to do was seek God, asking what was so wrong with him that he'd had to go to prison. He waved away most efforts to comfort him.

Friends had already been saying God would use Bo for good in jail. After all, that's who he was—a man who tended to bring Christ wherever he went. He didn't want to hear that, either. He was so deep in the wilderness of sorrow that he couldn't look up.

I could remember how, shortly before Bo entered prison, Ashley had predicted something like this might happen. She and I had made lists about how we thought prison might affect our family. She'd included this:

ASHLEY'S FEARS FOR GOD TO HOLD

I give Him my fear of Dad having to go to jail
because he always feels guilty for the smallest things,
and I think going to jail would make Dad feel a
burning pain for the rest of his life. It worries me

how Dad always thinks all the bad in the world is his fault and it's his responsibility to fix it. This is not healthy, and I think going to jail would make him go to the extreme and feel like he is not worthy to do the things God has planned for him.

She knew her father well.

I hoped, though, that Easter was a hint of better days to come. Andy, too, was hearing that Bo hadn't completely given up on serving God. During visitation one day, an inmate came up to him and said, "Thanks for giving us your dad for a while."

When Andy asked what he meant, the man told him that Bo had started a Bible study and had led many people to the Lord. At that moment everything about prison made sense to Andy. He suddenly understood why God had allowed this to happen to our family and especially to his dad. God had a greater purpose through this difficult time, and Andy's anger toward God just melted away. In its place, he was filled with peace.

Meanwhile, I continued to tell both of the kids that God was in control. I wanted them to have an eternal perspective— that life is all about forever, eternity. We had a daily choice: *Am I just going to be angry about this and pity myself? Or am I going to look to God?*

That was a moment-by-moment thing, and at any time I could have lost it. The thing that kept me focused was wanting to not waste the suffering. I told Bo, "If God is in control and you are here, there is a reason. We are not going to waste this suffering I'm going through, our kids are going through, and you're going through. It's so stressful. We're not going to waste it. We're going to find out what God wants to change in us—both of us. And why this has happened."

We were about to find out more.

I had no idea what the next phase of prison might hold. All I knew was that Bo would leave Camp Englewood the day God decided it was time—and His timing was always perfect.

CHAPTER 11

HALFWAY HOME

As we drove away from the prison on the day I moved to the halfway house, traffic startled me. Why were the cars going so fast? They seemed like weapons, missiles.

Had they always been that way? *I haven't been gone that long,* I told myself, gazing out the window. *But will I be able to get used to this again?*

For a couple of hours I was actually able to *go* home.

When Gari eased the van into our driveway, I could see a big, yellow, homemade, poster-board sign affixed to the garage door:

WELCOME HOME DAD

Two green balloons flanked the sign. The letters were green and red and blue, and embellished with hearts and stars— like so many of the cards Ashley had sent me in jail.

Gari, Andy, and I crouched in front of the sign so Ashley could take a photo. Gari and I held our two dogs. We all smiled. We all looked pretty tired, too.

And I felt strange. My home until an hour ago was a 10-by-13 room. Now as I walked into my house, all I wanted to do was unpack, settle into my chair, and return to normal life. But that still couldn't happen for four more months. Instead, my own true home was a place I could only visit occasionally for a few short hours in the days to come.

I still had to keep going, and as we headed for my next home in the halfway house, my weariness nearly matched my trepidation.

None of us really knew what might happen next.

Independence House

If the Detention Center had been like a heart attack and Camp Englewood had resembled quadruple bypass surgery, the halfway house was a blockage in three arteries requiring stents and a couple of nights in the hospital. All three were to be avoided if at all possible.

The Detention Center had offered nothing to do except sit in the cellblock and stare at the walls, talk to other inmates, or listen to the screaming. It was like a vise tightening on your head.

In the prison camp, you had the freedom to walk on the track or lift weights. The guards were always watching and the inmates were always dangerous, but the overcrowding wasn't as bad.

At the halfway house, you actually were able to work if you had a job. You could earn the privilege of going home once in a while, though you had to return at night. The halfway house was less intense—but it was still prison.

It was supposed to be safer, with more inmates who'd been convicted of nonviolent crimes. I guess it was. And you'd think everyone would obey all the rules, being so close to being free—not wanting to mess up and get sent back inside. But it didn't always work that way.

Like most halfway houses, Independence House was located in a residential neighborhood. Two stories, red and white brick, alley in back, tiny front yard. It stood on a corner at the edge of a series of storefront businesses. Three blocks away was East High School, the only school in Denver where I hadn't been able to get a hit when I was on the Thomas Jefferson High baseball team.

No sign identified Independence House. If you'd seen the 30 residents hanging out on the sidewalk, you might have thought twice—or assumed it was a fraternity.

The person in charge was the halfway house manager, George. His office was to the left when you walked through the front door. He was much like a prison guard, but not in uniform. He was tough as nails and followed the rules. He was friendly to me because I followed them too.

George was of medium build, cheerful, and usually mellow. He seemed interested in the inmates. As far as I knew he wasn't armed and didn't have a gun nearby. I figured that if there was trouble he'd call the U.S. Marshals.

Soon I learned that George and I had a mutual interest: golf. And he liked golf balls. He wouldn't let me *bribe* him with golf balls when I needed him to think of work I could do to earn more time at home. I did occasionally *inspire* him with golf balls to do that, however.

That was how it worked: Inmates could earn an hour or two at home on weekends by doing chores at the halfway house. That meant cleaning floors, pulling weeds, scrubbing walls, or vacuuming carpets.

I was anxious to earn as much time with Gari and the kids as I could. So I scrubbed the same floor, over and over, day after day. I did the same with the walls. It was, after all, a pretty small house. Pretty clean, too, the way I kept scouring it.

Family time became even more precious when I had to earn it. Before prison, I'd taken for granted freedoms like being with my wife and kids in my own home.

Now I cherished them.

Unfortunately, I hadn't earned any family time during my second night at the halfway house.

Even more unfortunate, that night—May 23—was our wedding anniversary.

I asked George whether the rules could be stretched to let us go out to dinner. He shook his head. I'd earned no work-release time, and he couldn't advance me any.

He would, however, allow us to park our minivan at the curb in front of Independence House, where he could keep an eye on me. If we could scrape some food together, we could have a picnic in the car.

Not exactly the celebration I'd hoped for, but it was better than nothing. We bought some bread and cold cuts and made sandwiches.

Opening the back hatch of the Voyager, I sighed. I'd had about a day and a half of feeling pretty good, thinking I was partway home. Now I was seeing again the pain I'd put my family through. Here we were, unable to celebrate our anniversary in anything close to a romantic way.

I'm not really out of their control, I thought. *I'm still in federal prison.*

During our picnic, Gari and I started discussing how I felt about going back to work and getting out in the community a little. All at once a tidal wave of emotions flooded my mind and heart. I began to cry uncontrollably.

Between sobs I tried to tell Gari that I was afraid of the future. I tried to explain that I hoped I'd learned all the lessons God wanted me to learn in prison. I wasn't sure I could handle being outside again. I feared I'd return to my old ways of trying to help everybody else and disappointing my family.

I wasn't very articulate. Gari kept saying, "Give me a word picture to describe why you're so emotional tonight."

Finally one came to me, and I did my best to share it.

"Let's say God gives us a dozen roses every morning," I began. "And He says, 'Here's what you're supposed to do. Go distribute these roses to everybody you come in contact with. That's what it means to live the Christian life.'"

I explained that in my mental picture God didn't seem to understand I was capable of handing out at least two dozen roses every day. So around the side of the house I had a little garden of my own. I'd take the roses He gave me, and then supplement them with another dozen. Then I'd spend the whole day like a lunatic trying to distribute the whole bunch.

I didn't want to go back to being that person. I was beginning to see that God knew what He was doing. I had my hands full just distributing the roses He'd given me. I didn't need to add more.

I wasn't sure my picture was clear, but Gari seemed to understand.

When our "celebration" was over, I'd cried for about three hours.

That made me feel even worse. I couldn't even make it through a talk over sandwiches without falling apart.

I'm still not really out, I thought.

Toeing the Line

Each time I was away from the halfway house and moved from one location to another, I had to place a call to George to notify him of my new location. He told the inmates that he could and would conduct surprise visits—to make certain we were exactly where we said we were, not off somewhere getting into trouble. Once again, I followed the rules to the letter.

Or intended to.

I blew it on my first full day out of the halfway house.

It was also my first morning back to work at the Anschutz Family Foundation in downtown Denver. I'd told George where I'd be.

Once in the office, I thought, *I need a haircut.* So at noon I went to see a nearby barber who'd been cutting my hair for years.

Seeing me, he said, "Hey, where have you been? I haven't seen you in months!"

I settled into his chair, and he draped an apron over my shoulders. "I've been in federal prison," I said, "and I'm still in federal prison."

"No, you're not," he said with a chuckle.

That's when I realized I'd forgotten to call George and tell him I was "on the move." Jumping out of the chair, I reached for the phone—all the while praying that I wouldn't be handcuffed and taken back to jail.

"I'll show you I'm in federal prison," I told the barber, and dialed George's number.

"George," I said sheepishly, "I have moved from the Anschutz Family Foundation office and I'm getting a haircut now. I forgot to call you, and I'm sorry."

He said, "That's okay. You'll get used to this. Do your best and don't worry about it this time."

I breathed a sigh of relief.

Or maybe two sighs. I was relieved that George hadn't read me the riot act—or worse. I seemed to be dealing with nicer authority figures now. George had a heart, not just a heavy hand.

But I was also encouraged by the fact that the barber hadn't known or believed that I'd been behind bars. Maybe there was a chance that my life would return to normal—someday.

I knew I was fortunate to have my part-time job at the Anschutz Family Foundation. Many Independence House residents had no job at all—and no prospects.

Worse, some of them seemed to have incredibly poor judgment. They'd sneak out at night, get drunk, and then get busted trying to sneak back in at 3:00 in the morning. Many times I witnessed one of the guys begging for forgiveness and a second chance as he was hauled off in handcuffs for doing something stupid. To be that close to freedom and mess up again was a risk I refused to take.

Gari told me she thought the halfway house was even more dangerous than prison camp, since guys would think, *I'm out!* They'd get careless and make mistakes.

I knew *I* wasn't out. *I'm still in federal prison here*, I reminded myself. *I'm in custody. I'm to report in. I'm to stay here.*

Sometimes I worried about whether the prison system might hold me responsible for what some other guy had done. I'd be lying in a room where an inmate had snuck out the window and think, *I hope I don't get in trouble for his actions.* Anxious to be released, I followed the rules and toed the line.

I was starting to see why the recidivism rate—the number of people returning to prison—was so high. Once you made it to the halfway house, what were you supposed to do? I had a job, a place to go, a family. But most guys just returned to their old habits.

They seemed to think, *I've got nothing else to do, so I'm gonna do what I did before. Now I know how the system works. Prison is dangerous, it's awkward, it's lonely, but you get a bed and get fed and you don't have to work. So I'm going back in.*

I felt sorry for guys I'd met who'd probably just end up behind bars again.

One Saturday, about a month after moving to the halfway house, I'd earned three hours at home by cleaning Independence House from top to bottom. I relished spending a chunk of the day with my family.

The time sped by. Not wanting to leave but knowing I had to, I said good-bye to Gari, Ashley, and Andy—a little later than I should have.

I had to be back at the halfway house by 4:00 p.m., which was check-in time for all the inmates. My watch told me I was cutting it close—too close.

Hoping to make it in time for curfew, I raced back.

At 3:55 p.m., just a few blocks from the halfway house, a Denver traffic cop pulled me over.

I groaned.

This time I'm in big trouble, I thought. George wouldn't overlook this one.

As the officer approached my window, I thought, *Well, be brutally honest here. Maybe this guy will drive to the halfway house, let you check in by 4:00 p.m. with George, and then write you a ticket when you're safely back in prison!*

With a sinking feeling I rolled my window down.

"Sir," I said, "I'm sorry I was speeding. But I'm a federal prisoner. I have to check in by 4:00 p.m. I don't know the consequences of being late, but they won't be good. If you could follow me just two blocks around the corner and give me a ticket in front of the halfway house, it would help."

The officer stared at me, a half-puzzled, half-amazed look on his face. Then there was a hint of a smile.

"Well," he said finally, "you don't look like a federal prisoner. And I can't imagine you'd make up that story. So get on your way—and slow down while you're at it."

"Thank you," I said. I knew that wasn't enough to express my relief and gratitude, but the clock was ticking. He returned to his squad car, and I drove off—making it just in time.

When my heart quit pounding so hard, I reflected on what had just happened. Once again I'd been treated with kindness by people in authority. And the policeman hadn't assumed I was guilty. *This guy actually believed what I told him*, I thought. *This is progress.*

Maybe there was hope for me. I didn't have to be defined by the FBI or my prison record. If a traffic cop was willing to give me a chance, maybe others would too.

It was a defining moment.

Not Myself

Understandably, friends and family wanted things to return to normal. So did I.

But there was something wrong—with me.

Before prison, most people had seemed to perceive me as a loud, confident, over-the-top individual and leader. But not anymore. Now they saw me as a guy who was crushed.

I could see why. Especially on the day I told Gari—and Helen and Everett Dye, who happened to be there—about a real estate opportunity. I believed it was a winner.

I was asked to raise the money for the transaction but I couldn't imagine doing it. The thought of risk-taking and figuring out the finances and making decisions was too much for me.

"My brain's not working," I told them. "I don't have confidence to do it. There's no way I would feel comfortable asking anyone to invest in this."

They said, in effect, "Please! You can do it! Come on! Wake up!"

But I shook my head. "No. I can't do it right now."

It was the same way when I was able to sit at a meal with my family. I'd be so happy to be home, even halfway. But when I'd look up, one of them would be staring at me.

"Why are you staring at me?" I'd ask.

Often the person would start crying, especially if it was Ashley. She or he would say, "I just want you to come home."

I'd say, "I *am* home!"

"No, you're not *fully* home."

So I wasn't truly myself yet. As Helen Dye said, there was still an underlying sadness about me that affected the way I looked, spoke, acted, and felt. It was a type of brokenness I'd never experienced.

Maybe this was a good thing, I thought. But I needed time. I wasn't ready to do a complicated real estate deal. I needed more time in the incubator.

It was a bit like being pregnant, I guessed. You could be tired of it and want to be done with it and want to rush through it. But only God knew the real timetable. Only He knew my true "out date"—the day when I'd be released from my underlying sadness.

I wasn't completely discouraged by the fact that I wasn't there yet. And I was honest about it, telling everybody I wasn't ready.

But some people didn't believe me.

From time to time when I was in the halfway house, I'd get a call from coach Bill McCartney, founder of Promise Keepers. He was trying to encourage me.

"Bo, get your head up," he'd say. "Quit looking at your past. Look to your future. Come to Boulder and speak to a men's group."

"Bill," I kept telling him, "I am not ready. I'm so broken, what I mostly do is cry. I go to work. I'm trying to function again. But I'm still in a halfway house. I'm not ready."

Later he'd call back and say, "You're ready. Let's go. Get up here and speak to this men's group. You're ready."

Coach McCartney being who he is, he finally talked me into it.

I walked into a Boulder restaurant early on a Saturday morning. It was a typical men's Bible study, with coffee and donuts and a guest speaker once in a while.

This time the speaker was me. I was supposed to have 35 minutes in front of 50 men, to share some of my story.

For 20 of the 35 minutes, I couldn't say a word. I was in tears.

They'd probably never had a speaker just stand there and cry in front of them. Occasionally I could muster the ability to say something, but most of the time I just stood quietly, silenced by humility and brokenness.

I thought, *What a waste of time for these poor men. They have to be miserable because I'm miserable.*

When I finished, Coach McCartney walked up front and put his arm around me.

"You're not ready!" he announced.

"Well, Bill, I think I tried to explain that to you," I said. "Thanks for recognizing it."

It was classic McCartney—he'd just been trying to love and encourage his friend.

I figured most of the guys in the room shared Bill's final assessment of my preparation level. It was probably the worst Bible study any of us—especially me—had ever attended.

But there was sympathy, friendship, and understanding, too. I could tell the guys were on my side. While I'd been trying to speak, there was mostly silence. But I could see that some of the men were crying with me.

If I'd been able, I would have told the group in those 35 minutes how my family and friends—and Christ—had stood with me. I'd have explained how I'd been zapped with an awful sentence because that's what God had in mind for me. It was a God deal. I was still on the bench, learning.

I hoped I was learning the lessons I was supposed to learn and could move forward with my life—someday.

Obviously that day hadn't arrived.

Finish Line

My mandatory release date—the day I'd be through with the prison system if I didn't mess up—was set for September 14. All that rule-following had rewarded me with the maximum amount of time off allowed for good behavior.

I—we—were limping toward the finish line.

As the date grew closer, Ashley gave me another card. On the front was a picture of a twisted highway. It said, "Life's Long and Winding Road."

Inside the printed message was, "Detours are only adventures in disguise."

Then she'd written this:

What an adventure you've had! Don't worry about getting back into everything. Everybody can't wait to have you back. And they'll love even more having the "new, improved" Bo. You've grown so much and I admire you for it, and I have grown with you.

I love U,
Ash

P.S. Smile

I tried, wishing I could share her certainty.

Gari's Story

When Bo was released from the prison camp, he was able to come home—sort of. It was strange because he couldn't stay.

We were still scared of what might happen next—what the government or some halfway house inmate might do. On that second night at the halfway house, when Bo and I had celebrated our anniversary in the van, I was glad that he wasn't literally behind bars anymore. But I could see in his face the devastation of his confinement. I guess he saw it in mine, too.

We just looked at each other and cried. We probably shared the same thought, too: *Okay, we're glad we're here, and happy anniversary. However, we're not exactly through with this yet.* It was sad leaving him that night.

I was actually more scared about his being in the halfway house than in prison. There was less oversight and more opportunities for guys to get in trouble. That trouble could spill over on Bo. I hated the whole thing.

They might bring drugs in, sneak out and get drunk, get weapons—who knew? Bo was in a place with these potentially dangerous people and his safety depended on their actions. Were they violent people? I didn't know, so we kept asking the Lord to protect him.

Bo's release was a great relief, and I looked forward to restarting our lives. As soon as Bo was home, life went back to normal for Andy. I was glad he didn't have to be the man of the house anymore and that Ashley could return to her sophomore year at the University of Kansas.

But Bo was a wreck and would need a long time to heal. We had to put one foot in front of the other, and found that re-entry can have its own tough moments.

CHAPTER 12

RELEASED
BUT NOT RESTORED

For Gari and me, the new normal looked like a long, slow process of trying to come back to life. It seemed we would be in a state of confusion for months—if not longer.

I continued to catch Ashley staring at me with the strangest look on her face. I'd ask, "Why are you looking at me like that?"

She would say, "I just want you to come home."

I *was* home. But I was so broken that the real me was lost somewhere, and she could see it in my face.

I felt I was in a good place with the Lord and was extremely grateful to be back with my family. But personally I was crushed.

For one thing, we were financially in a hole. Not wanting

that hole to grow any deeper, I knew I had to find another part-time job soon. My half-time position with the Anschutz Family Foundation was a blessing but couldn't support us. I was willing to try anything.

Then there was the feeling that Gari and I had lost our way socially. We didn't know where we fit in. We didn't attend the church I had resigned from because we didn't feel accepted there anymore. I was no longer involved with Promise Keepers, and Gari had resigned from the national board of Mothers of Preschoolers. We didn't have the same circles of friends anymore because we no longer were connected to the same organizations.

We struggled with how to relate to the few who'd turned their backs on us while I was in prison. Being loyal had always been important to me. When people were disloyal, I still loved them—but I chose to love them from across the street. I'd think, *I've seen you when the bullets fly, and you're not there to help.* I tried not to judge their motives, though.

The problem wasn't that all of our acquaintances rejected us; in fact our close friends became even closer. It was partly that we weren't up to the challenge of socializing. There was a long stretch when we didn't feel like going out for dinner or a movie, and we could sense it was awkward for others too. They didn't really know what to say to us or what they could do.

Feeling isolated, we circled the wagons as a family and tried to regroup. Survival became our single-word focus.

As for me, I really didn't feel like being part of anything. I didn't want to go anywhere. I didn't know where I belonged.

That's why, when my friends Dan and Phil pushed me into joining them for a golf tournament in Las Vegas, I felt awkward. The tournament was sponsored by the Colorado Golf Association, and men from all over the state were gathering for three days of golf and fellowship. I wasn't sure I'd fit in.

My time with Dan and Phil was great as usual, but I didn't know the Lord had a pleasant surprise waiting for me that would alter my life in many ways.

I was waiting to tee off on the golf course one day when a guy named Joe Coors approached me. I'd met him, but we didn't really know each other all that well. Putting a hand on each side of my face, he moved in close. "I am glad you are here," he said. "There are a lot of us in Denver who know you got a rotten deal. And we are glad to see you getting back on your feet."

Wow! I thought. *What a gift.* Overwhelmed by his kindness and acceptance, I began to cry.

Joe had just the right touch, at just the right moment, with just the right words. We would go on to become lifelong friends, as did Gari and Joe's wife, Gail.

A few people, though, were at the other end of the spectrum. One former friend didn't help much when he told me I "changed the dynamic" when I was around, so I "wasn't wanted."

I didn't want to be a problem to others. *Just don't go anywhere*, I told myself. I wasn't hiding; I was recovering. And I didn't feel like answering questions.

Gari kept telling me, "You should see a counselor, somebody

who could help you." I'd had bad experiences with counselors who'd betrayed confidences, and didn't want another one.

What I did want was to be part of things where I wasn't looked down on as an ex-convict—or merely tolerated. Fortunately, there were things to do—when I could find the strength.

Job Hunting

Around that time I was offered a great job.

The president of the company was excited; I knew I could do what was needed. It seemed to be a perfect fit. I went to a formal meeting with the board of directors to make it official.

During the meeting the president declared, "We voted 7 to 1 for you to join us, and we're excited to have you."

I frowned. Somebody hadn't wanted me to come. That bothered me.

I said, "Would the one person who voted no mind telling me why you voted no?"

A lady raised her hand. "All I need to know about you to know I don't like you," she said, "is that you went to federal prison."

Maybe I shouldn't have been so sensitive because we really needed the income; maybe I should have been less direct. But I wanted to be honest. "All I need to know about this place to know that I don't want to work here," I said quietly but firmly, "is that she's here. I want to go where I'm welcomed, not merely tolerated."

Respectfully declining, I walked out of the room.

The president hustled after me, asking me to reconsider.

I wouldn't budge. I told myself, *She was here first. This is her dream. She's on the board of this company. She has a right to the joy she feels coming in here without having to deal with an individual just out of federal prison.*

But I thought something else, too—about how I'd allowed the FBI, a few critics like this woman, and my prison record to define who I was. I wanted to say, "Wait a minute. That's part of who I am. It's not going to fully define me. I'm going to get off the pine, come back, and do something with my life to God's glory and not my own. I don't need any more trophies, I don't need any more championship rings. I've got enough successes. I just need to feel good about serving the Lord."

It was a rousing mental speech. The truth was, though, that I was having a hard time feeling good about anything.

I was still crying at least once every day.

Sometimes I cried when I was with my family. There were also many breakfast appointments when I would just start weeping. A good friend named Doug Sauter would sit there with me in a restaurant booth, seeming to understand that I wasn't crying about anything in particular, but everything in general.

There was no denying it: This shift to being an ex-con—wearing that label—was painful.

At one of those breakfasts, a friend said, "I found this Scripture. I thought it would encourage you." He read Proverbs 26:2: "An undeserved curse does not come to rest."

In my friend's eyes, prison had been an undeserved curse. Now it had been lifted.

I thanked him, saying the verse did encourage me.

But for the moment I identified more with a popular song I'd heard on the radio. It was called "Learning to Live Again," and one stanza went like this:

I'm gonna smile my best smile
And I'm gonna laugh like it's going out of style
Look into her eyes and pray that she don't see
That learning to live again is killing me.[15]

There's my story, I thought as soon as I heard it. I felt the same as whoever wrote that last line: I was making progress in adjusting to life after prison, but that adjustment was taking its toll.

Being an ex-con, it appeared, might turn out to be a life sentence.

In the Red

There was no arguing with the numbers. Our family was in serious financial trouble, hundreds of thousands of dollars in the hole because of past unsuccessful real estate deals.

Gari and I refused to file for bankruptcy. We'd always paid our bills and wanted to continue that policy. The problem was how to do it.

We agreed that we'd do whatever it took. The first step was to start selling our possessions.

Anything with commercial value, we sold. We sold our home and moved into a rental. We sold our two late-model cars and started driving two that weren't worth much more than $1,000 each. Gari's sister Ali and her husband helped us by purchasing the few pieces of art we owned. They didn't need the art but knew we needed the money. We appreciated their kindness.

Eventually we sold the diamond from Gari's wedding ring. That was the worst. I already felt I'd let her down, and now it seemed we couldn't sink any lower. Gari was more than willing to take that step, but it felt extreme and disheartening. I knew it was my fault.

Determined not to fall any deeper in debt, I was anxious to get to work and break even as quickly as possible. My brain didn't seem to be functioning at all, but I had to try. I remembered a little poem I'd learned about faith and action. I didn't know who'd written it, but it seemed appropriate:

> *Blessings come from heaven,*
> *But there's something you should know;*
> *If you're praying for potatoes,*
> *You'd best pick up the hoe.*

Ever since I'd left the halfway house I'd usually felt like crying, not working. Now I thought, *Here's the arrangement: You want God to bless you? Then get to work. Do your part.*

Bible verses came to mind such as "If a man will not work,

he shall not eat " (2 Thessalonians 3:10) and "All hard work brings a profit, but mere talk leads only to poverty" (Proverbs 14:23). They made me think, *What I need to do is get in my car and drive—even if it's through tears—to wherever I can work.*

Even as I drove around looking for work, on most days I wanted to pull my car over to the side of the road and cry for a while. But I felt I owed it to my family to try every day to make ends meet. I'd pray every morning that the debt wouldn't be with us forever.

As glad as I was to be home, the prison of financial strain was almost as bad as the one with the gray bars. The pressure never let up—never even seemed to quiet down for a day or two. I would go to work, pray, think, and try my best, hoping for a breakthrough.

Finally, in addition to working for the Anschutz Family Foundation and broadcasting high school football games on the weekends, I went to work selling aluminum roofs.

My job was to go door to door in neighborhoods all over Denver and Boulder, trying to find potential customers. Since I was almost completely clueless about home repair—let alone construction—I was way out of my league as a roof salesman.

One day I was offering a man a 25-year guarantee on a roof.

He said, "Well, I'm 75 years old. I'm not sure this guarantee is of interest to me."

"Oh," I said. "Good point." I paused, thinking. Then I asked, "Has anyone ever talked to you about eternity?"

"No," he said.

"So you haven't ever thought much about faith or spiritual things?"

"Not really."

"Would you be open to you and your wife talking with me about those topics right now?"

He said, "Yeah. We'd be very interested in that."

So I shared the gospel with them—and they both prayed to receive Christ!

They also bought a roof.

Later they told the owner of the company what had happened. He called me into his office.

He looked a bit amused. "You're actually a little more interested in and a little better trained for sharing Christ with people than selling aluminum roofs, aren't you?" he asked.

"Definitely," I admitted.

That's when he and I agreed to start thinking about whether I had a viable future as a roof salesman.

I was thankful to have that job and saw God's hand in getting it. Still, I was frustrated every day, and continued to feel sad. I would ask the Lord, *Are You sure this is what I'm supposed to be doing? Because I sure don't feel like I know what I'm doing. I don't feel like I'm very good at it.*

The sadness would hit me like a flood, unpredictably. I'd think, *This is what my life is now. I'm doing the best I can, but it sure doesn't feel right. It just feels difficult.*

But I'd push through that and keep working. I thought, *Maybe God can steer a moving car better than a parked car.*

So I kept moving, trying to do whatever He gave me to do.

Hearing of our situation, several friends stepped up. Some helped financially, like Verley and Pearleen Sangster. Verley had been a regional Young Life leader and president of the Center for Urban Theological Studies in Philadelphia. A veteran minister and respected member of the African-American community, he was loyal and reliable.

Gari and I had helped the Sangsters buy a home once. Now, about a month after I'd left the halfway house, this couple mailed us a check for $2,000. It came with a note: "Word on the street is the brother has been making 11 cents an hour. Thought you could use a little boost. Glad you're home."

I called Verley and said, "Hey, with eight kids you don't have an extra $2,000."

He said, "That money has your name on it. Use it however you want to."

It was a real expression of support and love—and we *did* need it.

Many others helped too. Phil Anschutz, along with his wife, Nancy, and his sister, Sue Anschutz-Rogers, continued to stand by us. And when we had to sell our house, Doug and Kathy Sauter made it easier by purchasing a home for us and allowing us to rent it from them. An engineer and a contractor, Doug took that small, older house and turned it into a palace for us.

My sister, Lana, and her husband, Charlie, continued to give us money, regularly pray for us, and encourage us on days when we were falling apart. So did a host of others.

Some friends helped with advice. Our friend Bobb Biehl urged me to create and maintain a list of personal positive accomplishments. The purpose: to remind me, as often as needed, that even though I was experiencing a down time, my entire life hadn't been negative.

And then there was Helen Dye, whose parenting advice had once turned my life around. She knew about my desire to be everybody's hero, my seeming inability to tell anybody no, and how those habits had gotten me in trouble. She told me, "Bo, because of your enthusiasm and your wisdom and your ability to speak, you promise more than it is healthy for you to deliver when you're exhorting or encouraging someone. They think when you say that to them, that means you're going to do it, and then you go ahead and do. That's not good for them and it's definitely not good for you."

So when someone wanted to meet with me about raising money for a project—which usually meant asking me to do it—I needed to avoid becoming entangled in their proposal. Helen said, "You should just not take the meeting."

Once again, she was right.

There were many changes I knew I should make, having had plenty of time in prison to think about them. I'd made some commitments to myself, in case I ever got out and had a life again. But to keep them I'd need all the help I could get—from friends and from the Lord.

God Is Able

One day I watched Atlanta pastor Charles Stanley on TV. His sermon that day was entitled, "God Is Able!"

It turned out to be exactly what I needed to hear.

The famed pastor's points were that God is able to save us (Hebrews 7:25), establish us (Romans 16:25), help us (Hebrews 2:18), keep us from falling (Jude 1:24), make grace abound toward us (2 Corinthians 9:6-8), save us from the fire (Daniel 3:17-18), humble us (Daniel 4:33-35, 37), and use us (Ephesians 2:8-10).

As I listened, I began to see that God—and only God—was able to do everything. I wasn't able to do much at all.

That came as something of a shock. For years I'd had a pretty high view of my abilities, thinking I was doing God a favor to use them for Him. I'd been a competitor, a producer, a hero. Charles Stanley was saying that I was full of it. I hadn't been able to do any of those things I was so proud of—starting churches and ministries and hitting baseballs and sinking free throws.

Only God was able.

Often I'd thought I was the reason why successful things happened. But God was able, not me.

I had more than my share of failures mixed in, of course. But overall I told myself, *Bo, you are able to get the job done for God, and God is smart to choose you to help!*

What an arrogant thought! It was now hard to believe anything good was accomplished with me in the way. Only God's grace and provision had made things happen; I'd been *way* off in my thinking and leadership style.

I had a wire crossed in thinking that my role was more

important than anyone else's. It was just as important to vacuum the carpet at church as it was to buy the carpet in the first place.

Just as coming into a relationship with Christ hadn't been based on my strengths, neither was how I served Him. If He chose to use me, great; but my role was to do my best while giving all the credit to Him.

Sitting there watching the televised service, I wondered whether the biggest mistake of my life had been thinking I was in some way able to help God by starting summer camps and local TV shows. Who did I think I was?

I'd missed the truth by a mile. I knew I'd better not forget it. I needed to work as if it were up to me, but let Him use me for His glory and not mine. After all, Jesus had said, "Apart from me you can do nothing" (John 15:5).

I thought, *Yeah, you can still do some good. But get the perspective right here. It's God who's able to do these things through you. It's not you doing anything independent of Him.*

I never meant to be a glory hog or a show-off. But I'm sure there were some people who saw me that way. Maybe they had a point.

I thanked Charles Stanley and God for the revelation. If Bo was able to do anything, it was only because God was able to do everything.

The best part was that it wasn't just a chastening thought. It was freeing.

Since success wasn't about me, I didn't need to feel the

pressure of being everybody's hero and the solution to everybody's problems. People needed to see God as their solution and their hero, not me!

I took notes on that sermon. It helped me understand that if someday God wanted to do something, He might use me. Maybe I would be off the bench eventually. Maybe I'd be used to do some God things.

Maybe.

Moving Mountains

As my recovery continued, my list of needed changes lengthened.

One shift I wanted to make was to stop being reckless. Too often I'd been climbing to the top of the temple and jumping off—putting God to a foolish test.

I promised Gari I'd be more cautious. There'd be no more hurried, 10-minute meetings where I signed papers as I had for the "straw borrowing" loans.

So I put together a "personal protection team" I'd consult before doing anything in business. It included Gari, an attorney, an accountant, a bookkeeper, and two friends who'd given me wise counsel.

Before prison, I'd thought there was something to be gained from moving fast. I'd assumed thinking and acting quickly were rare but needed talents. The new me thought recklessness wasn't a good quality at all. It was just ego, pride, self-effort—even showing off.

Now, instead of rushing, I'd say, "No, I need to pray about that and talk with my personal protection team."

Sometimes people resisted. "Well, I need to move faster than that," they'd say.

It took a while, but eventually I became comfortable with saying, "Good. Go ahead. But you're going without me."

I'd learned that fast didn't work.

Another habit I needed to form was asking more questions.

Before prison, I might ask a prospective ministry or business partner three or four questions—the most pertinent being, "Are you a Christian? Do you know the Lord?"

If someone said yes to that, I figured it told me most of what I needed to know. As the "straw borrowing" fiasco proved, that was a good way to get burned.

My natural style had been to lead with my heart and engage my head later. I learned the hard way that having your head and your heart in balance was a good thing for everybody concerned.

So after prison, I thought, *There's no harm in asking 25 questions and learning about the person, the deal, whatever you're looking at.* I learned to ask a whole *lot* of questions.

In addition to asking questions of other people, I was learning to ask a few of myself. One was, "Who is ministering *with* us, and who are we ministering *to*?"

I hadn't asked that about the banker who'd wanted me to borrow money. I thought we were Christian brothers in business and ministry together.

But after he acted the way he did, I realized I should have been ministering *to* him, not *with* him. Apparently he didn't know Christ—or at least his actions seemed to indicate that he probably didn't.

I knew Scripture called that kind of mismatched partnership being unequally "yoked" (2 Corinthians 6:14). Being naive and overly optimistic weren't valid excuses for the mistake I'd made. Even behind bars I'd started thinking, *I need to know who's with me and who I'm ministering to. When I get out of prison, who do I want to invest my time with? And who have I wasted enough time on?*

That didn't mean I wasn't planning to hang around people who didn't know Christ. It meant I'd keep my eyes open to what other people's belief systems really were.

Another change I wanted to make was to stop playing to the crowd.

I'd seen plenty of basketball players who'd had that problem. They'd try too many fancy moves just to entertain the fans—a behind-the-back pass or an acrobatic hammer dunk. It was easy to tell when a player was oriented toward something other than winning as a team.

I'd had the same problem—maybe not on the basketball court, but in my whole approach to life. For years I'd caused my family, my friends, and myself a great deal of suffering because I oriented my life toward *project*s and *people*. I was performing for the wrong audiences. I was driven by these goals and other people's needs—not by Christ and His lordship in my life.

I needed to live to please Christ in what I said and did. I started to focus on the question, "Would Christ approve of what I'm doing?"

Too often my project orientation had led me to use poor leadership skills with people. I'd hurt many along the way, usually unintentionally. Now I was seeing that God's people and my love for them was much more important than any project.

When I thought about all the changes I needed to make, I wondered whether God and I would ever manage to move this mountain. Sometimes, though, I found reasons to hope.

One turned up at a Promise Keepers event the summer after I was released from prison. I ran into Coach Bill McCartney again, who apparently was still speaking to me in spite of all the tears I shed in front of his men's group.

Bill looked at me and said, "There was a worldliness about you before prison, Bo, that is not present anymore. And I'm glad it's gone."

I knew the kind of worldliness he was talking about—flirting with attractions like Cherry Hills Country Club, and the seduction of money.

I was relieved he could see a difference in me.

One change down, a few thousand more to go.

Lessons Learned

Coach McCartney's encouraging words were a big help. But it pained me to remember the day in Boulder when I'd wept uncontrollably at that speaking engagement. Ever since, I'd been reluctant to try public speaking again.

But then came another invitation. It was from a pastor in Denver, asking me to talk to his church's men's group. I didn't know if I was ready. But finally I said yes.

Sitting down with paper and pen, I pondered what to say. I thought, *I'll just talk about what I'm living right now.* Freshest on my mind were some of the lessons I'd learned in prison.

I called it "12 Tips So Men Can Win." I even worked some rhymes in, making each tip a sort of catchphrase that guys could memorize.

But as the appointed date approached, I wondered whether I could pull this off. Could I function in front of a group, or would I have another meltdown?

The evening of reckoning arrived. I was introduced and stepped to the front of the room, my heart thudding in my chest. I was supposed to talk for about 45 minutes. After a few introductory remarks, I glanced at my notes and began:

1. *Don't take too long to admit when you are wrong* (1 John 1:8). I told the group that when it came to prison, I wasn't a victim. Things hadn't gone too well for me in the judicial system, but I'd also made some bad choices that put me behind bars. So this tip meant, "Own up to your side of the deal." When you find yourself in a mess, ask yourself what mistakes you made that contributed to it.

2. *Identify, confess, and forget your sin; He died on the Cross so you could win* (1 John 1:9-10). I explained that if you were too hard on yourself, wallowing in the fact that you did something wrong wasn't good either. Identify what you did wrong, confess it to the Lord, and accept His forgiveness. No matter how much I'd messed up by making wrong decisions relating to ego and pride, I'd seen firsthand that God was in the business of fresh starts and second chances.

3. *You can overcome anything—if your faith is in the King* (John 3:3; 2 Corinthians 5:17). The object of your faith, I said, is a critical component. You could have faith that you'd start this year in center field for the Colorado Rockies—only to get a reality check when you realized you were 50 years old and had never been able to hit, run, or throw. Putting your faith in the King of the universe was safe, smart, and secure.

4. *To avoid a mental riot, get alone with God and be quiet* (Philippians 4:6-7). I described how, before prison, there was too much clutter in my mind. I took on too many things at a time, and ran constantly at a pace that wasn't healthy. Prison was the first place I could really get quiet and learn what God was teaching me.

5. *Read your Bible every day, or soon there might be hell to pay* (Hebrews 4:12). Prison was also the first place I could sit still and read Scripture—two, three, sometimes four

hours a day. I told the guys how I'd talked to Chuck Colson about how the Bible-reading habit could change once you're back in the real world; Chuck and I had agreed that when you got out of prison you tended to fall back into a pace that wasn't healthy spiritually. We couldn't pinpoint the reasons. Maybe in prison we were more anxious to search the Scriptures because our needs were so great.

6. *Every single day, take the time to pray!* (1 Thessalonians 5:16-18). I mentioned how, in prison, my good friend Carl and I would do our Sunday morning exercise walk. Circling around the track for about two hours, we'd pray for each inmate in the camp—roughly a hundred guys. We did so out loud with our eyes open, praying for them by name, for specific things we knew were going on in their lives. Most weren't Christians, so we prayed for their salvation. There was time to *listen* to God, too, as I sat quietly in my metal chair in the corner of our room or walked around the track.

7. *To set your heart and mind on things above, concentrate on building your ladder of love* (Matthew 22:37-39; Colossians 3:12). I noted that when Bob Beltz and I started doing marriage retreats around 1980, we'd taught that the Scripture about loving the Lord with heart, soul, and mind laid out His order of relational priorities for us. Number one, Christ; number two, self; number three, family; number four, friends; number

five, one's fellow man. We'd described it as a ladder with five rungs. In prison I was able to think seriously about those priorities and how to live them.

8. *Honor your wife every day of your life!* (Ephesians 5:25). I explained how Gari had gone above and beyond what would be expected of a wife when I was in prison. We not only remained married; our marriage improved as well. Now I chose my words more carefully when I talked to her, and was committed to my personal protection team—of which she was the captain. She'd become more of a partner in everything we did.

9. *The law of the harvest you should know; you'll eventually reap the seeds that you sow* (Galatians 6:7-8). This is more or less what I'd said to my kids in Phil Anschutz's conference room before going into court for my hearing. "It's harvesttime, and some of this harvest is already bad. But there will be good parts to this harvest also." I told the men that the seeds we'd sown in friendship reaped a bountiful harvest in prison, as evidenced by the letters and support we received. I'd contributed to the negative harvest by planting bad seeds, making bad choices. I'd done too much, too fast, too arrogantly.

10. *Take daily action to communicate; write, call, encourage—love in action is great!* (James 2:17). Having experienced

this 137-day period where I'd written letters and sat at visitation, deeply communicating with family and friends, I felt even more responsible to "catch someone in the act of doing something good and tell them about it." I admitted to the guys that I hadn't always stopped to say, "You're doing a good job," or "You have the right personality for this." Now I tried to do it daily.

11. *Do not get entangled in worldly affairs; keeping things simple will limit your cares* (2 Timothy 2:4). The last couple of years had taught me that simplicity could protect me from dangers I didn't even know were lurking. Now I didn't want to do needlessly complicated and entangling things like borrowing money for friends or from a bank for that matter, or forming partnerships with people I didn't know well. Not counting the cost up front had set me up for problems.

12. *No matter how deep you are in the hole, remember that God is still in control* (Revelation 4:2). I told the men that in prison, incredible peace would come from thinking, *I'm sitting in the stairwell here, in a federal prison cellblock, but I still don't doubt God's in control.* I'd prayed that I would learn all the lessons I could through this experience. I believed that how you conducted yourself in The Hole affected how soon you'd get out of it. When you commited to the Lord, even in prison you could see God's power released.

And then I was done.

I'd cried a few times during the talk, briefly. But this time, the message had been delivered.

I sat down, relieved that the Boulder disaster appeared to be behind me. The group and the pastor seemed happy with what I had to say, and I was happy to have said it in a way that didn't leave anybody sobbing—especially me.

It was a small step, but it seemed to be in the right direction.

Making Progress

Some things were looking up.

Ashley was having a great time back at the University of Kansas, earning good grades. Andy had been offered a full scholarship to play football at the University of Colorado, which made us all very proud and happy.

Well, I told myself, *you haven't completely disrupted your children's lives.*

My job situation, though, was another matter.

I'd been selling aluminum roofs for about six months. I'd done the best I could. I'd done it faithfully, anyway—and the boss seemed pleased with me.

I wasn't pleased, though. I was miserable.

About that time I got a call from my friend Richard Beach. His organization, Doulos Ministries—which specialized in discipling, training, and placing Christian servant leaders to help youth and their families—was having a problem. Doulos was a little short every year of raising the funds to meet its budget. In fact, at the moment they were in such bad shape that their employees were five paychecks behind.

Richard asked me to fly to Branson, Missouri, with him to help.

Soon I was sitting with the board of directors. For an hour and a half we discussed possible solutions.

Suddenly the chairman of the board asked me to step out of the room.

"Have I done something wrong?" I asked.

"Quite the contrary," he said. "You've done something right. But we need a private discussion here."

When I returned to the room, the board offered to hire me as a consultant. I was asked whether I could raise a certain amount of money to help the ministry with its financial problems. I believed that with God's help, I could.

It was the first time anyone had treated me that way. It felt good.

For decades I'd been asked to raise money for Christian causes—but always as a volunteer. It had never crossed my mind that someone might *pay* me for what I'd been trained for 20 years to do, since the time I'd quit pro baseball and worked as a fund-raiser at the University of Colorado.

The board and I came to an agreement. I became a part-time fund-raiser instead of a part-time salesman of aluminum roofs. Richard and the ministry and I did well together, and eventually we caught up on those paychecks.

It was a great blessing for my family. Counting the

part-time job with the Anschutz Family Foundation, we could now meet our income needs.

In my euphoria, I told Gari, "We're getting back off the bench."

But in my darker moments, I wasn't so sure.

Despite my progress, I still managed to cry every day.

About a year after my release from prison, I finally decided to see a counselor. A friend recommended a lady named Mary.

Going into the first session, I was doubtful. After the two bad experiences I'd had with counselors, I wasn't exactly filled with trust. But I couldn't stomach the endless emotional roller coaster anymore.

"Mary," I said, "I'm sick of the sound of my own voice. I'm sick of my story. So the sooner you start talking, the sooner I can quiet down and stop explaining all this—and the more likely it is I'll come back here for a second visit."

About 20 minutes into that first appointment, she said, "Okay, you can stop. I can help you."

"How's that?" I asked.

"Have you ever read a book called *Boundaries*?"

"Never heard of it," I said. "But the word intrigues me."

She told me about the book by Drs. Henry Cloud and John Townsend. It had been published while I was in prison. Setting boundaries, Mary explained, was learning to say no—not taking on every project that came my way. Just hearing her description made me feel a little better.

Then she said, "You're really not very good at setting

boundaries for yourself. Consequently, you're probably not very good at letting other people set boundaries for themselves."

It was the first time I really understood that saying no could be a good thing. It was a way to protect myself and my family.

Nobody else was going to do that for me. I was used to attending meetings and hearing things like, "We need to raise $2 million. So how are we going to do it?"

"Well," I'd say, "there are 20 of us. Why don't we each raise $100,000?"

"No, that doesn't work. Why don't you raise a million and a half, Bo, and the other 19 of us will raise the other $500,000?"

I didn't have time for that, and I didn't have two hours a day every week for people to pick my brain about their next ministry vision. I knew that at the end of every meeting they'd ask, "Can you give me a list of your friends I can call and ask for money?"

"No," I'd have to answer. As Helen Dye had suggested, better I should say that word in the beginning to avoid those meetings entirely.

I needed to say "no" to other requests too. In the 1970s and 1980s, one former friend would call me every few months and say, "My wife and I have overdrawn our account by $1,500 or so. Could you cover it for us?"

Since he was in tears and was my friend, I'd gift him the money and do it again when he called the next time. Things like this would happen with others, too, over and over. All of that needed to stop!

So *Boundaries* helped. When I read it, I saw that I'd been at everybody's beck and call. That wasn't how I was supposed to operate. *I'm called to serve Christ*, I reminded myself. *I'm not called to be the answer to everyone's problems.*

Later, Mary helped me with another insight. One day she asked, "What word would you use to describe yourself, Bo?"

"*Misunderstood*," I replied. "Can you help me understand why I'm so misunderstood?"

She paused, then nodded, "Yeah. You're tall, you're smart, you're well-spoken, you're loud, you process quickly, and you're successful. To some people, that's just overpowering."

She hesitated, then continued. "I think, now that I know you, that all you've ever tried to do is empower people. So where the misunderstanding comes is that you're trying to *em*power, and people get *over*powered."

I pondered that for a moment. "So how can I get better?"

"Well, when you say 'could,' or 'should,' that puts the power in your possession and is overpowering the other person," she said. "If you slow down and say, 'Would you be interested in my opinion?' and they say, 'Yes, I would,' then they've invited you to give them your opinion."

I thought of an example immediately. I could recall how my kids had reacted to my unsolicited advice.

When Andy was in tenth grade, I'd said, "You should be a big-time college kicker and punter. You don't even have to get better. All you have to do is get more consistent. And you could take it all the way to a full scholarship at a big school."

In Andy's case that had worked fine; he'd taken it as encouragement. He'd said, in essence, "I'm putting my shoes on right now and I'm gonna go kick!"

But it hadn't worked with Ashley. If I said, "You should be in the lead role in the school play because you have a better voice and more stage presence than that other girl, and you could be in any play you wanted to try out for," she'd do exactly the opposite.

"Really?" she'd say sarcastically. "Well, thank you, Dad. Now I'll go out for the tennis team instead. I'm not even going to *do* the school play."

I'd overpowered her—and probably a lot of other people. I sighed. *Another lesson to learn.*

How would I ever learn everything I was supposed to, much less apply it? This business of being refined never seemed to end—though I was beginning to wish it would.

On the Radio

Ever since the day I'd been sentenced, Jim Dobson had been nudging Gari and me to be guests on his *Focus on the Family* radio broadcast. He'd wanted us to do it even before I'd gone to prison, but we'd felt overwhelmed by everything else. He'd wanted us to do it while I was behind bars, to record the program at Camp Englewood itself. Now, in the spring of 1994, he was asking again.

This time we said yes. I was reluctant, knowing how close to the surface my emotions still were, and how I was struggling to learn the right lessons. I'd managed to make it through "12 Tips So Men Can Win" at the church in Denver, but this was different. I didn't feel ready. And I knew Jim had a way of encouraging people to share their feelings on his show.

Sure enough, I choked up frequently during the interview. And my answers seemed too long to me.

As I'd told my counselor, I was sick of my story, sick of hearing my own voice. And sick of crying.

The broadcast received a good response from listeners. A prison inmate wrote this in a letter:

Dear Bo and Gari,

I am currently serving a six-month sentence in the [county jail] for commission of various offenses. . . . On March 9, 1994, I heard your interview on the Focus on the Family program. I just want you to know how much that program meant to me. My wife was also listening to the program at our home.

Your testimony helped me develop a new relationship with Jesus Christ. This new strength has given me the encouragement and inspiration to look to a new beginning. As I learn more about God's unconditional love, I am discovering how to be accountable and to accept the subsequent discipline involved. I have also learned to replace my pride with humility and meekness. It is for this reason that I am glad my mistakes and deceit were finally discovered. Without this failure, I would still be controlled by pride and not the grace of God. With the help of the Lord, I will become the person I want to be, an honorable and responsible man. My past mistakes and failures will have a meaning.

Then there was this, from another inmate:

No, it is not pleasant how we are transformed into the image of Christ, but if we will trust, adhere, rely on His voice, guidance, and will to do what He deems necessary, then God will open the door to His power. I don't know you, have never met you, and never even heard of you before today, but brother, if you will seek God with all your strength, He will give you a vision of His will. He will burn it into your heart, and nothing else will matter. There's a work the Master is bidding you to do. "Seek and you shall find."

But I was tired of seeking. Tired of finding. Tired of explaining. Most of all, I was tired of crying.

I'd been crying practically every day for nearly three years.

It seemed I'd never be able to escape the weight of my imprisonment, the underlying sadness that wouldn't go away.

I'd been making some changes. But if I was going to survive emotionally, mentally, spiritually, and maybe even physically, I was going to have to make one more.

It was a big one.

Gari's Story

Many friends stepped up to help our family before and after Bo was released from prison. Some gave money, some brought food, some called, some wrote Bo letters. This meant the world to us.

One example of this incredible support came from a man named Dave, who attended our church. He was in a group of people who gathered weekly to pray for our family.

Every couple of weeks Dave would call me to get a report and ask, "How can we help you?"

I'd have all this amazing stuff to tell him—ways in which God had provided something, or protected Bo and the rest of us, or sent a whisper that He was still in control.

Dave would say, "I call to encourage you, and all you do is encourage me!"

I told him, "Well, God is here. And He is with us, and He is sustaining us. And you're part of that with your prayers."

As for our struggle to relate to the few former friends who'd made things harder for us when Bo was in prison, that was tough for Andy and Ashley, too.

Psychologists say that all anger comes from a deep hurt, and I think Bo's imprisonment and the disloyalty of certain people hurt us all deeply, especially Andy. Our children were loyal; they didn't like the man who admitted saying untrue things to hurt Bo during the prison days. They didn't even want to hear the man's name.

I would just say, "It's not your battle. You need to let it go."

That wasn't easy, and this situation was extremely painful for our family.

I knew it was also painful for Bo to take the job selling aluminum roofs so he could support the family. I appreciated him doing anything. He has always been a hard worker.

When it came to all the changes Bo had made and continued to make, I could see many of them. I became number one on his priority list—partly because he needed me so much and I needed him, too. But to tell the truth, it was a little hard to get used to having someone care so much. I'd never had that before in my life. But it lasted.

I'd already decided that I needed to act as normal as possible even if I didn't feel that way. Bo and I did the best we could for the next three years—the rebuilding years.

I wasn't improving physically too much during that time, but I was able to function to some degree. Bo kept working hard, and we both enjoyed our kids and their activities. We'd always been their best cheering squad and celebrated their successes.

I tried hard to create a climate in our home that made it a sanctuary from the pressures of the world. Since life was at times chaotic when I was growing up, I wanted people to feel comfort, calmness, and security when they were in our house—even if Bo and I didn't always feel that way as we lived through this period.

When we started selling things to stay afloat, my world didn't come crashing down.

In other words, selling my wedding ring wasn't quite the emotional experience one might assume. To Bo it was. But to me, at that point, it was just *stuff.* We needed to get Ashley through college, and I was thankful we had so many things we could sell.

Naturally I wanted things to return to normal, but Bo still had that underlying sadness.

I knew he was doing the best he could. But it was a sad time; neither Bo's emotions nor his mind seemed to be operating normally. Helen would ask him, "Can't you just get *out* of this?"

I remember driving around one day with Bo. He said, "You see that property right there?"

"Yeah," I said.

"If I was in good shape, I would be doing a business deal on that, make some money. But I can't even think clearly."

He probably wished I was better too. With me operating at perhaps 50 percent of capacity, things were much harder for him.

For us, this period was a watershed. There was Before Prison and After Prison.

I kept hoping that After Prison would be the better part. Sometimes, though, I had to wonder. But I always believed we'd see light at the end of this tunnel.

CHAPTER 13

NEVER BETTER

By August 1, 1994, I'd had it.

I'd cried long enough.

Part of me was waking up and feeling okay, but part of me was still broken. I'd start each day depressed, thinking, *Well, I don't want to go where I'm not welcome. I don't want to impose my problems on somebody else.* It was that underlying sadness Helen Dye had talked about.

Some of it came from the pain of going to prison. Some came from letting others define me solely as an ex-convict. The rest came from believing that things were miserable and bound to get worse.

When I thought about the shame of being behind bars, I realized it wasn't shameful to have what Gari had called an "Enforced Spiritual Retreat." I'd been sifted (Luke 22:31).

One of the things I learned from Charles Stanley's "God Is Able" sermon was that God controlled the method, intensity, and duration of the sifting.

When I realized that, a feeling of comfort settled over me like a warm quilt. *Okay*, I thought. *Prison wasn't an accident. The handpicked method of sifting I just experienced—and my wife and kids, who were also sifted—was federal prison.*

As for duration and intensity, it had never been worse than I could stand—though it came close a few times. And it had an ending—if I would *let* it end.

The pain of my story still weighed me down, though I was learning the lessons God had for me. Almost daily I felt compelled to tell everyone about my time in prison. It became a sort of calling card. I talked about it too much, as if it were the defining moment of my life.

I was beginning to see that I had to draw a line in the sand and say, "I think I've learned what I needed to learn. I need to move on and head in another direction." If I didn't, my mess would remain a mess rather than become my message. This short chapter of my life might go on forever.

When it came to letting others define me—I thought of how the FBI, the U.S. Attorney's Office, and the judge had decided I was a criminal. Even a local leader had told people while I was in prison, "Bo's a liar." Over the years I'd bought that man and his wife two cars, paid for the remodeling of their house, and more—most of which he either denied, or said he'd forgotten about. It occurred to me that he was the one who had trouble remembering the truth—not me.

Now I thought, *No. I'm not gonna let the FBI define who I am, much less this guy. I'll take into account what they said, and prison is a moment in my life. But it's not the defining moment.*

As for believing my situation was terrible and getting worse—I considered the rock-bottom truth. Christ had gone to the Cross to pay for my sin, and I would have a happy ending if I sought God's forgiveness—which I had. Romans 8:28 said God would work all things together for good. That was a happy ending too.

I'd also been forgetting the whole idea of grace. I'd been thinking, *I'm a mess and don't deserve God's love; the scoreboard shows me as a total zero. Why would God want me?* But His arms were open wide.

I knew that grace meant unmerited favor. There was no scoreboard for grace. I couldn't win or lose God's love. That was a *really* happy ending.

I needed a booster shot to stop the way I'd been thinking. Maybe the booster for me would be better information.

So when that day in August came, I woke up and thought, *I've cried long enough. I'm tired of this, my family's tired of this, my friends are tired of this. I need to turn a corner by feeding myself a thought that will help me stay upbeat, energetic, positive.*

I came up with a plan.

If anyone asks me how I am today, I decided, *I'm gonna say,* "Never better."

I couldn't remember hearing the phrase anywhere; it just came to me as a positive thing to say.

If I say, "Never better" and they ask, "Why?" I'll say, "This is my best day ever because I've decided it is, in Christ."

And if they say, "That sounds crazy," I'm gonna say, "Well, if you run into me tomorrow, tomorrow's gonna be even better than today."

I was ready to be happy. I thought this might jump-start the process. It just came to me: *This is a good day to start being happier.*

It seemed natural. Before prison my attitude had been pretty much 100 percent positive. But I'd felt buried alive for a long time.

The day had come to put things in the right perspective: "God's in control, you're His man, this all happened for good reasons, and you've learned your lessons. Quit browbeating yourself. Get up and have a good day."

It was time to start stating the facts. And one fact was that, thanks to God's work during my year or so on the bench, I was a more obedient person than I'd been before I'd gone to prison.

"Never better" was also a much shorter, sweeter answer than the ones I'd been giving.

Was it motivational hype? Maybe. But it was also mental food I needed to feed myself so I could heal.

Would it work? I was about to find out.

Good Medicine

An old adage says, "Most people are about as happy as they make up their minds to be."

Turns out it is true.

The first time I tried "Never better," it seemed to make people smile. They said, "That's good! I'm glad for you!" Or, "I wish I had that."

Everybody seemed to think it was funny, especially family. But they liked it.

To my surprise, the underlying sadness disappeared quickly. In just a week I was doing . . . better.

Did I believe it when I started saying it? Not exactly. But soon it became a self-fulfilling prophecy.

I found myself saying those two words over and over, to all kinds of people. Some said, "Wow, that's a good response. What do you mean by that?" That led to further discussions.

I had heard many times as an athlete that you move in the direction of your self-talk, and you could never rise above your own words. Also, I had been coached that if you wanted your results to improve, you had to change your words. So "Never better" was helping me to do that.

But mainly it was medicine, designed to put me on the right track every day by focusing on God, the things of His Kingdom, and the fact that "Never better" was a good place to be.

This is my best day, I would think, *and tomorrow's going to be even better. Why? Because of what Christ did on the Cross, because of what He's done in my life, and because I say so!*

As I began to climb out of my version of The Hole, I realized more and more that nobody had been sitting around thinking about my problems as much as I had. Everybody had difficulties, and mine were no worse than anybody else's.

"Never better" was starting to look like a profound shift in the healing part of my whole journey. With each passing day I grew more positive and excited as I fed myself better information. I had to stop wallowing in the method of sifting God had chosen for me. It was time to celebrate that I'd paid attention, that I hadn't wasted my pain. With the help of friends and family, I was beginning to feel better.

Despite having God's Spirit in me and knowing plenty of Scripture, I needed the "Never better" declaration to push me over the top. It was the tool I chose to remind myself, *This is a good thing you just went through. These are good lessons you learned. Everybody else may think you're crazy, but even though you can't pay your bills, you're in debt, you and Gari are driving two automobiles that barely function, and you're selling everything in your house to make ends meet, you need to start expressing outwardly what you're feeling inwardly—that it's a good day.*

This wasn't "Fake it 'til you make it," or "Smile more and you'll feel happier," or "Name it and claim it." This was about counting my blessings and being more grateful for what I had.

It also gave me perspective. I focused on things that were better and deeper than before—marriage, family, friendships, and most of all, my relationship with Christ.

I found plenty of biblical support for the idea. For example,

Philippians 2:5-7 (ESV) says: "Have this mind among your-
selves, which is yours in Christ Jesus, who, though he was in
the form of God, did not count equality with God a thing
to be grasped, but emptied himself, by taking the form of a
servant, being born in the likeness of men."

The idea of having the mind of Christ appealed to me. My
mind had been cluttered with a mix of prison and pain and
healing and "God's in control" and "I must be a bad person."

And 1 John 1:9 tells us: "If we confess our sins, he is faithful and just and will forgive us our sins and purify us from
all unrighteousness." Having gone through that process, I
should have known that I had a clean slate and been able to
get past this. But I hadn't managed to make it all fit together.

"Never better" helped me show outwardly what I was trying to become inside—a person who'd been forgiven. If we
believe in Christ, I thought, we should all be "Never better"
all the time.

"Never better" was working for me, so I kept it up.

My good friend Phil Irwin later described in writing how
well things were going:

Although it took a few years of rebuilding his life,
his finances, and his confidence, Bo became an ever-
stronger Bo. I remember the day he said, "I'm tired
of being sad." He chose to be happy even under the
sad circumstances he faced and was still living with.
The answer to the everyday question of "How are
you?" no matter how he really felt was and still is,

"Never better!" Since then Bo has created incredible successes not only in his personal and family life but also in his business life. I'm more proud than ever to call Bo Mitchell a friend and brother for life.

Eventually saying "Never better" became as natural to me as breathing. I said it every day to everybody I greeted and still do. People started telling me, "I know what you're going to say, but I'll ask anyway." And many of them said it back to me.

The phrase seemed to be an example of what Bobb Biehl called a "brain-brander." It could be a Scripture, a short quote, or a phrase you memorized. When it popped into your brain it could encourage, teach, and inspire you. It was like the four-word instruction a baseball coach had once given me on swinging a bat: "Short, quick, and down." Whenever I entered the batter's box I would think of the words he'd branded on my brain.

In the same way, "Never better" flooded my mind with a thousand positive thoughts about what Christ had done for my family and me. It was a reminder that every day is a blessing from God and that Christ is ultimately victorious.

Did that mean I was immune to trouble or failure? No. But I knew that spending eternity with Jesus would be my final outcome!

I don't know what might have happened if I hadn't started saying "Never better." Would I have stopped getting up, moving forward, going to work, being productive, and celebrating the lessons I'd learned from God? Maybe I would have chosen to feel sorry for myself and be crippled emotionally forever. Perhaps I would have been immobilized by anger, barely creeping through life.

"Never better" helped turn off that underlying sadness and move to the improved version of myself.

That phrase, and the message it delivered to me, brought to mind a verse in Exodus. Moses and the Israelites were shaking in their sandals, paralyzed at the water's edge as the Egyptians closed in on them. "Then the Lord said to Moses, 'Quit praying and get the people moving! Forward, march!'" (14:15, TLB).

It was time for them to get off the bench.

And now it was finally time for me to do the same.

Grace and Mercy

Soon I found my mental fuzziness and uncertainty fading. It was time to get our family on its feet financially. I continued my work with Doulos Ministries and the Anschutz Family Foundation but began to add a few helpful jobs in addition.

In 1995 the Furniture Row Companies hired me to speak to its employees about leadership, communication skills, teamwork, and similar subjects. It wasn't a ministry, but it was a great job. For the next several years I did quite a bit of speaking, and there were years when I would have 125 speeches scheduled by January 1 for that calendar year alone.

For a long time Gari had been telling me, "You're a really good public speaker."

I'd think, *That's nice, but so what?* It hadn't helped our family much. All my speaking, like my fund-raising for ministries, had been volunteer work.

Now both were financially rewarding. It was affirming, too; my ex-convict status didn't seem to stand in the way. The people who hired me and listened to me appeared to accept me. I worked for Furniture Row for 12 years.

It was something to be thankful for. So was what happened next.

We were still thousands of dollars in debt—and still refusing to declare bankruptcy because Gari and I didn't believe that would be right for us.

About that time a friend named Ted Blank called me and said, "I want to help you and Gari get out of debt." I didn't know Ted very well but had always considered him a great guy and a good businessman. I was surprised he even knew we were in debt, and even more surprised he wanted to help us.

For the next few months Ted shared many investment opportunities with me, none of which appealed to me for various reasons. Then one day at lunch he showed me something that would change both of our financial lives forever.

There was an opportunity to buy a certain property— Mercy Hospital in Denver. Ironically, it was located only a few blocks from the halfway house I'd lived in before being released from prison.

As Ted and I tried to find a way to make the transaction work, I kept noticing the sign on the top of the facility. It didn't say Mercy Hospital.

It just said Mercy.

That made it a constant reminder of what God had shown me—mercy as well as grace. I'd always been taught that grace was getting what you don't deserve, and mercy is *not* getting what you *do* deserve.

I'd look at the Mercy sign and think, *I hear your message, Lord! I hear it, and I'm finally beginning to understand!*

It was also a reminder of the teaching that God was *able* and I wasn't. Determined not to revert to old habits and think I was able, I worked as hard on the hospital deal as I'd worked on anything in my life, and Ted did the same. Yet I knew this wasn't my doing; it was the Lord's. He was reaching His hand out to us and giving us a gift.

Or at least He would be if the transaction worked out. It was a very unusual case.

Ted and I repeated many times to each other during the formative stages of the transaction that "God is in control and His timing is perfect." It became our "go to" theme when things would get difficult. But for the most part, the deal came together beautifully because the Sisters of Charity, who owned the hospital, needed to move quickly so they could meet some important deadlines they were facing. Ted and I were willing to meet their needs to move fast, and in God's mercy, we were able to purchase the hospital. We raised the necessary funds to complete the purchase in a way that was beneficial for the Sisters of Charity and for us. A true win for both sides of the transaction!

Many advisers from the medical field told us we stood to gain a greater profit if we held on to the hospital for a few years. Ted and I chose, however, to sell the property within one year at a fair price to the right buyer. Even after we split the proceeds, the transaction was the godsend that put our family back on its feet. I will forever be thankful to Ted for his friendship and hard work in making the Mercy deal available to us.

Gari and I were able to pay the taxes that we owed on our gain, make a generous gift to some local charities—including a 10 percent tithe and more—and then pay off all of our outstanding debt—and more, including the $2,000 that we'd received from the Sangster family during our darkest financial time.

When Verley received his check, he protested, "That wasn't a loan!"

I said, "Well, this isn't *payback* of a loan. Yours was a gift, and this is a gift."

After all, God had given mercy to us.

The sale of Mercy Hospital also allowed us to repay family members and friends who'd helped us financially. Whenever I saw the Mercy sign after that, I was reminded that, from start to finish, the Blanks and the Mitchells had been blessed.

I thought, *God is allowing me to put into practice the lessons I learned in prison, as well as the lessons I learned by doing business the wrong way in the past.* I was glad to honor Him by trying to do it the right way.

It was the first time I'd really felt completely off the bench.

Good-bye Pine Time

For me, the end of pine time couldn't just mean making business deals. It meant charitable and ministry ventures too. At least I hoped it would.

I wasn't sure, though, whether people would accept that kind of leadership from an ex-con. Would they keep their distance, as some already had? Or would my post-prison experience be like Chuck Colson's?

When Chuck ended up in prison after a high-profile post in the White House, his former career was toast. But God had called him to serve prisoners and then a whole nation. Chuck said that the real legacy of his life was his biggest failure—that he was an ex-convict. His great humiliation— being sent to prison—was the beginning of God's greatest use of his life. His words inspired me!

So far I'd kept my ambitions pretty low. Frankly, when I was released from prison I thought I'd just mow lawns, drive an old car, and learn to be happy the rest of my life just trying to pay my bills and live.

I also knew I'd had a problem with pride when I'd tried ministry and charity work before. Besides trying too hard and doing everything in my own strength, I'd often thought my contribution was more complex and maybe more valuable than anyone else's.

By allowing me to go to prison, the Lord had followed up big-time on James 4:6: "God opposes the proud but gives grace to the humble."

I didn't want to get on the slope of pride again. Don't get me wrong—I was proud of my kids, my marriage, and some things we'd accomplished. But that wasn't pride in my contributions or myself. It was more of a team-oriented, body-of-Christ joy.

Did I still want to do well in everything? Yes. But partnerships and teamwork were much more important to me now. So was having a more reasonable pace. Christ's pace had been marvelous, something to behold. He was never rushed, never followed the spotlight.

I wanted to be more like that. And I was about to get the chance.

In the summer of 1996 I got a call from a friend who introduced me to Dan Roberts. A singer and songwriter, Dan worked with a country music star. My friend said Dan had told him that this singer and his band were touring and had scheduled a stop in Denver. They wanted to play some baseball while they were in town. Was I up for that?

I said yes. I spent a few hours at Coors Field, chasing fly balls and helping Dan and the band get in some batting practice. It was fun, but I didn't think much more about it.

Six months later Dan called again. He wanted to know if this music star could ask me some business questions.

"Sure," I said.

So the star called our house, and I was able to help him with a contact he was seeking. Before long, we'd struck up a friendship and he told me he'd wanted to experience Major League Baseball because he loved the game.

A year later, when the famous singer was thinking about retiring from touring, I asked him to help me start a charity. "We could help some kids and you could get a taste of Major League Baseball at the same time," I told him.

We began praying about it. Since 1979 Gari and I had wanted to start an organization that would raise money for other charities, and now we wondered whether this might be it.

It was. On January 7, 1999, we stood at a press conference at the Hotel del Coronado in San Diego and launched the Touch 'Em All Foundation. Soon we renamed it Teammates for Kids.

I served as president for seven years, and over the next decade we raised tens of millions of dollars. The Foundation's activities involved more than 2,000 professional athletes as well as corporate sponsors. We also organized special events honoring the kids we helped, our donors, and our players. It was a blessing to see the foundation grow and help so many people.

It also felt peculiar to be running a national foundation for a famous singer, given my ex-convict status. But my ego had been so thoroughly squashed in prison that it allowed me to interact with some other big egos and not get swept up into it. I had set boundaries, and our staff and board members were all great people. With teamwork, the organization was very successful.

Still, I was careful to be up front about my past. When I had a chance to do business with someone as part of the foundation's work, I'd give that person a copy of the Focus on the Family broadcast CD that contained the interview with Gari and me.

"Listen to this," I'd say. "If you want to do business with us, you should know that the president and cofounder went to prison."

That fact continued to make a difference to a few people, even at my uncle Waldo's funeral in a small Oklahoma town. After saying hello to most of the people at the church, I felt blessed to see family members I hadn't seen in years.

My happiness changed to sadness, though, when an elderly woman approached me and asked, "Aren't you Margaret's boy who wanted to be a minister but ended up going to prison instead?"

Not certain how to respond, I just said, "Yes, that's me." It was funny and sad all at the same time.

I thought, *There it is again. I'll never escape the ex-con label. Not even in little Cordell, Oklahoma—800 miles from home!*

The New Me

In the spring of 2004, Chuck Colson called and said he was considering stepping aside and hiring a president for Prison Fellowship, located in Virginia, near Washington, D.C. He didn't exactly offer me the job but asked whether I'd entertain the idea.

I didn't quite say no, but I did express my doubts. By that time Gari and I were grandparents, and Gari liked living close to the kids.

When the call ended without resolving the issue, I did think about it.

On the one hand, it sounded like such a good opportunity. The old me, the one with the big ego, would have immediately said, "Sure. Let's explore this together." After all, here was an internationally famous guy asking me to consider leading his organization, rattling off complimentary reasons why he thought I could do a good job for him. I appreciated that.

But the new me couldn't seem to entertain the idea. I said, "Chuck, God will have to make this awfully clear to me for me to even consider it—because this doesn't feel like a fit." After all, I was already the president of a national organization.

As we discussed the specifics of the job, I seemed to be passing the test. I liked that, too.

But perhaps the most powerful reason to pursue the position was the potential to turn my prison record into a plus. I thought, *Here would be the best reason I've heard of for going to prison. I went because it prepared me to help Chuck at Prison Fellowship.* When I thought about that, I started to cry. Taking that job would seem to publicly validate what our whole family had been through.

My main concerns were mostly family-oriented. My priorities were my wife, children, and grandchildren. Gari liked Colorado. And to be honest, life in Washington, D.C., wasn't of great interest to me, either.

It took me only a few days to discuss this idea with my personal protection team and decide that the timing was not right for us. I thanked Chuck and felt good about the team process we'd gone through to make the decision.

Even though there was a new me, the past resurfaced a few years later when an article appeared in the *Denver Post* on October 21, 2008. Reading the headline "Nottingham Resigns Amid Probe" blasted loose an avalanche of memories and mixed feelings.

Judge Nottingham, of course, was the one who'd sentenced me to federal prison.

The article, written by Felisa Cardona, started this way: "A series of sexually charged allegations over the past year, including a recent claim by a prostitute that Chief U.S. District Judge Edward W. Nottingham Jr. had asked her to mislead judicial investigators about their weekly trysts, prompted Nottingham to resign his lifetime commission Tuesday."[16]

According to the newspaper, Nottingham was being investigated for misconduct by Chief Judge Robert Henry of the 10th U.S. Circuit Court of Appeals. This probably wasn't the way Nottingham wanted to end his career.

In the weeks to come, several people called Gari and me, asking, "Do you feel vindicated?"

The answer was no. We felt bad for the guy. We didn't celebrate that he'd made a mess of things.

Next came a call from Focus on the Family. A vice president from the fund-raising department came to see me. He wanted to know whether I'd emcee Focus donor events at The Broadmoor hotel in Colorado Springs. He said Dr. Dobson had requested I do that "from now on" because people liked me and appreciated my humor.

They also wanted Gari and me to give our testimonies at the events. That included the prison days.

We said yes.

When we spoke at those events, we'd say, "Bo went to prison, and we made it through stronger than ever because of Christ, our commitment to each other, and communication."

When we were finished, people would open up and want to discuss the darker sides of their own lives—their marriages, their businesses. Gari and I would spend entire weekends consulting with people from all over the country who could identify with us. It was an honor.

Eventually Focus asked me to consult with the ministry's fund-raising team. Their leadership was entrusting us with their donors, and their faith in us meant a great deal.

I had a similar feeling the day a man called me from Geneva College in Pennsylvania. The school wanted to give me an honorary doctorate.

I hesitated. Finally I asked, "Does your board know I've been to federal prison?"

"Yes," he said. "That's not why we're giving you a doctoral degree. We're giving it to you for all the great things you've done in your life. We're aware of your legal history, but that's not a consideration."

His answer made me feel welcomed, humbled, and celebrated all at the same time. I knew now that the Lord was responsible for anything worthwhile I'd been involved in, but it still felt good. Once I'd thought prison had wiped out anything decent I'd ever done, but I was glad to be proven wrong.

From Gray to White

One day we received a phone call from a surprising source: the White House. As best I can recall, this wasn't long after George W. Bush took office in 2001.

Matt, a social secretary at the White House, called to ask whether Gari and I could come to a meeting about faith-based initiatives.

I suspected it was a mistake. "Hey," I said. "Have you looked up my past in your computer lately?"

There was a pause as he checked my record.

"Oh," he said, sounding a little embarrassed. "I forgot you went to prison."

That didn't bother me. In fact, it made me feel good that he'd forgotten. For so long I'd assumed "went to prison" was all anybody thought about me.

His voice was kind as he asked another question. "Would you wait for the next invitation?"

That was okay with me.

I didn't know whether we'd ever receive another, but we did. In 2002 First Lady Laura Bush threw a 60-couple Valentine's Day party for the president, and we were invited.

I had to admit it was fun. I was thinking, *We're accepted again and we're welcome at the White House! The government that made us feel unwelcome by sentencing me to prison is now making us feel more than welcome. Another whisper from God!*

By God's grace I'd gone from the Gray-Bar Hotel to the White House. We didn't know who had put us on the guest list or why, but it was an honor.

Another invitation came when Teammates for Kids raised money for Little League's Challenger Division, a program for kids with physical and mental disabilities. Gari and I were invited to attend the league's baseball game on the South Lawn of the White House.

President Bush was there, watching the game. I knew he was a baseball fan; after all, he'd been a part owner of the Texas Rangers team. When I had a chance to talk with him, I was amazed to learn that when the president was a little boy he'd met my father. He knew all about my dad and his baseball career. He knew his career batting average and all about the strikeout to end the perfect game. The president even told me my dad was one of his childhood heroes!

More Ministry

Things continued to improve for us. To centralize and better organize the various ministries I was involved with, in 2005 I formed Crosswalk Fellowship. It started with Bible studies and special events, and eventually gave birth to several other ministries that functioned under the Crosswalk umbrella.

One of the first was Game Day Memories, which purchases tickets for sporting events in 15 stadiums and arenas around the country and distributes the tickets at no charge to families with children who have special needs.

In many cases, the parents of these kids have been round-the-clock caregivers since the day their children were born. Game Day Memories allows them to enjoy a few hours "off the clock."

Crosswalk Fellowship has also helped two churches purchase buildings for their congregations. The building our ministry owned from 2010 to 2014, called Crosswalk Center, housed a messianic Jewish congregation, a Korean church, a Russian church, a Scottish church, and a Pakistani church all at the same 75,000-square-foot facility. Talk about a ministry center! We had it covered.

Susie Hayes has provided the directional leadership for Crosswalk Fellowship as its president and Mark Klibbe, Jayne Conant, and Gari complete our small staff. Together we serve a lot of people and have grown into a successful ministry. Bob Beltz and I even reentered the radio business with a weekly show called *You Get the Blessing*. We interview people in ministry, allowing them to share their faith in Christ and any need their organizations might have. My job as cohost is easy since I still consider Bob the smartest man in the world!

The support and friendship of the Crosswalk Fellowship staff, board members, and participants has been extremely affirming to Gari and me. God has continued to show me that He can, in fact, make use of me. Especially the new and transformed version of me!

Free at Last

Finally, there was a call in 2012 from the Colorado Rockies baseball organization—and a job offer. Fifty-six years prior to the phone call, I had watched my dad strike out to end the only perfect game pitched in World Series history. I'd seen my dad deal with that famous 1956 strikeout with class and dignity. He did not let it slow him down for long.

With God's help, I hadn't let my strikeout stop me for long, either—but I did let it change me.

Now I was entering the Rockies clubhouse as a consultant to help improve an already great culture. I was told to report at 10:00 a.m., January 6, to start my new job. That sounded familiar. Exactly 20 years before, at the exact time of day, I had self-committed to federal prison. Showing up for this appointment was definitely more gratifying. Yet my personal strikeout had taught me many lessons that prepared me for this job.

I'll never be the man I was before I went to prison, and

I never want to be. I say "no" frequently to requests for my time. I'm not reckless, and when my life gets too busy with too many strings attached to me, I readjust and change.

The Lord taught me how to be free in Him.

He also taught my family a few lessons while I was incarcerated.

One day, several years after my release, Andy interviewed Ashley about the experience on a local radio program he hosted. Here's a portion of what Ashley shared:

I look at our lives and how much they've changed for the better. Like you said, we were on cruise control. It did seem like everything was perfect, like everything just came to us and worked out, and then all of a sudden, *bang!* Everything hit. I'm so glad, because I don't want to be the kind of Christian who's on cruise control. I want to be shaken. I want the Lord to say, *Listen, you guys are strong and I need you to wake up so that you can see there are other people out here who are in prison, other people who are sick.* So not only did our family become closer and Dad and I became friends, it got us ready to go out in the world more and say, "I'm going to show you who I am. I'm opening up my heart. I'm not perfect; in fact, I'm very far from perfect. This is what I've been through."

And because Andy had also experienced God's care during that time, he shared this:

Keep in mind that the Lord has your interests and your goals and your biggest dreams in mind every day of your life. It may not seem that way, but He always does. He'll always take care of you, and He'll always see you through.

It was clear that our kids were learning lessons too. Gari remembered the message God gave to her as I was sentenced to prison: "This will be the salvation of your children." Was this what God had meant?

The trials changed *everyone* in our family, including Gari. She'll tell you that she developed a deeper faith—partly because of my imprisonment and partly because of her illness.

Beginning in the late 1990s, Gari finally recovered enough to resume more of her life. In 1997 Gari and I started a couples' group called the Colorado Council for the National Day of Prayer. This group helps support the National Day of Prayer Task Force with finances and other resources. The great friends Gari made there and in other groups have been wonderful for her after so many years of being isolated because of her illness.

In 2000 Gari was asked to serve as a Mothers of Preschoolers mentor at Cherry Hills Community Church and served in that position for 10 years, and she also works with inner-city ministries.

"With all the things I've become part of, my life is healthy and fulfilled," she says. "I'm not fully recovered; I think that will come about in heaven. But I'm so very grateful for all I have," she says. "So did God bring us to the place of abundance He promised me the first night Bo was in prison (Psalm 66:10-12)? I don't know what your definition of abundance is. But for me, it's what our lives are today."

> For you, O God, tested us;
> you refined us like silver.
> You brought us into prison
> and laid burdens on our backs.
> You let men ride over our heads;
> we went through fire and water,
> but you brought us to a place of abundance.
>
> PSALM 66:10-12

All the new opportunities and Gari's improved health were tremendous blessings, but the best by far was our growing family.

When our daughter, Ashley, married Andy Larson, and our son, Andy, married Dana Evans, it was like life was starting all over again.

And now that we have four beautiful grandchildren, Gari and I feel God has blessed us beyond belief. When the grandkids are all together, it is an endless time of laughter and joy.

When my grandson, Mitchell, and I play catch, I remember my days as a boy when my dad called me his "running mate."

At those times I can almost hear snatches of a hit song from the early '60s, sung by Paul Petersen. It was called "My Dad":

When I was small I felt 10 feet tall
When I walked by his side
And everyone would say, "That's his son,"
My heart would burst with pride . . .[17]

I'd loved my father. I tried to please him, but sometimes I tried too hard.

I'd done the same thing with my heavenly Father—with similar results.

All that effort, all that pain. All those tears.

It had taken a prison sentence to show me that self-effort and accomplishments would never be enough.

And that, thanks to God's grace, they never had to be.

At long last, I was finally free.

The Reason Why

I WENT BACK TO PRISON THE OTHER DAY.

Not as an inmate, but as a visitor.

I'd tried to return 12 years before, making it as far as the office at the entrance—where the guards turned me away when they learned I'd been an inmate.

Now I was trying again. As I walked toward that concrete fortress, I felt awkward, sad, weighed down by the memory of how Gari and Ashley and Andy had gone in and out of that place nearly every day to visit me.

Almost 23 years had passed, but it seemed I'd been trapped here yesterday. I could smell the food and feel the despair. The thought that I'd actually been locked behind these walls was so overwhelming it almost took my breath away.

I stepped up to the front desk in the little office, mindful of the gray-barred door behind it. One uniformed guard sat at the desk; another stood nearby.

This time I didn't volunteer that I'd been here before, much less which side of the door I'd been on. I simply introduced myself as chaplain of the Colorado Rockies, which was true.

That made all the difference, of course. The guards smiled, happy to answer my questions.

"Do the inmates still run the business office?" I asked.

The guard at the desk looked puzzled. "Well, they *clean* it," he said. I recalled how that had been our first assignment every morning—before we paid the bills. Sharing that detail, I decided, might not be a good idea.

I asked about employees I remembered—Julie from the Cold Room, administrator Mr. Swanson, the lady who ran the business office. The names rang no bells with the guards. It was all ancient history.

Those people were all gone. Or at least they'd gone on with their lives. *I'm glad I've gone on with my life too*, I thought.

I asked whether the chaplain was around. His assistant was, and the guards called him. When he showed up, we chatted. I couldn't tell whether he was more like Chaplain Halsey or Chaplain Del.

When I asked whether I could go inside, I was told I couldn't on short notice. There were forms I'd have to fill out in advance.

That was okay. I'd seen enough.

Thanking the guards and the chaplain's assistant for their time, I promised to look into getting them tickets to a Rockies game.

As I left the prison that day, I felt happiness mixed with heaviness. I could see the faces of the friends I'd met there, remember their stories. And I was glad I'd made the best I could of my time there, trying to let God refine me.

I drove slowly out of the parking lot. Through the side window I saw the flagpole I'd walked around and around in my attempt to exercise.

I had one more place to visit: the halfway house.

It would be the first time since I'd left. Thinking I remembered the address, I pulled up to an intersection in a residential downtown neighborhood and saw a building that definitely wasn't Independence House. But it didn't look new enough to be a replacement.

Confused, I wandered down the block. I remembered some of the storefronts. This had to be the right neighborhood.

I asked a man on the sidewalk if he knew where Independence House was. He'd never heard of it but looked it up on his smartphone. Sure enough, I was just a block or two away. Time and I had mixed up the address.

Finally I reached the two-story brick residence I remembered. In front was the parking space where Gari and I had spent our wedding anniversary, eaten sandwiches, and shed all those tears.

Four young men hung around on the sidewalk. Some were smoking. There were a lot of tattoos.

They turned out to be three inmates and a security guy who looked like he could have been one too. I told them I'd lived there once.

One asked me, "Did you used to work here?"

"No," I said. "I was an inmate."

"You don't look like an inmate," said another. "What do you do?"

I said I was a minister—which was also true.

"I *thought* you were," the guy with the most tattoos said.

I asked him whether he had a faith of his own.

He hesitated as the smoke rose from his cigarette. "I . . . kind of lost my spirituality in prison," he said finally. I could hear the regret in his voice, and my heart went out to him.

"We all need jobs," another guy said.

My heart went out to all of them. "If I owned a company, I'd hire you," I said. I knew the odds were overwhelming that without work, these men would go back to their old habits— and back behind bars.

Looking at the second floor where my room had been, I asked the security guy if I could take a look inside to see whether the house had changed. He shook his head. Somebody had to approve that, and she wasn't around.

I tried to say something encouraging to the inmates, but it sounded a little hollow. I left thinking, *Well, I can pray for those guys because I know what to pray for.* But I also felt that heaviness, that sadness that they had to be there.

It was hard to believe I'd been there too. Over the years I'd sometimes ask myself, *Did prison really happen?* Often it seemed like a dream, and not a good one. If nothing else, visiting Independence House gave me tangible evidence that I hadn't made the whole thing up.

Lately I'd been thinking a lot about prison. Feelings were resurfacing, along with unanswered questions. Sometimes it was hard to sleep.

One night I found myself up at 2:00 a.m. A question that had nagged me for a long time was back, and suddenly I had the urge to answer it more clearly and succinctly than I had before. Finding a pen and paper, I wrote quickly. The words seemed to flow without effort.

Five minutes later I was finished. Feeling at peace, I put the pen down, climbed back into bed, and fell asleep.

The next morning I looked at what I'd written:

Did I go to prison because I had a bad lawyer who didn't even read the documents pertaining to my case because he thought it was all a big joke?

Did I go because the FBI was ordered by some big shot in Washington, D.C., to make sure "heads were going to roll" in Denver because of the savings and loan crisis?

Did I go because I was a naive fool to ever have a single conversation with the FBI, much less be aggressively forthcoming?

Did I go because a renegade judge decided to make an example of me since he believed in "general deterrence"?

*Did I go so Grady, Blaine, Peter, and a few others
could receive Christ as their Lord and Savior?*

*Did I go so my wife and children would see that
their husband and dad needed them—and that he
was flawed like everyone else in the world and not
to be put too high on a pedestal?*

*Did I go to rid myself of partners and friends who
weren't loyal to me in the first place and only liked
me when my style benefited them?*

*Did I go so others who followed after me for
the same offense would not have to suffer the
judges' wrath and would fight the system and win
because they witnessed what truth and honesty
had earned me?*

*Did I go so I'd have a more meaningful testimony
for the rest of my life when I was asked to speak at
churches or retreats?*

Obviously, the answer to all of those questions, from my point of view, is a solid "Maybe."

But even stronger than any of those, I believe I went to prison so my roots could sink into the deep soil of faith in Jesus Christ—the only meaningful purpose in anyone's life.

God is in control and His timing is perfect! I went to prison not because God brought this evil into my life, for that is against His very nature—but because He allowed it to happen for my own good and for the good of my family and friends.

Now it makes perfect sense to me. If I'd known that even one day in prison was a possibility, I would have fought the government tooth and nail. I probably would have walked free.

If so, I would have missed all the lessons I learned in prison. It had to go exactly the way it went. I lost 36 pounds and a few so-called friends, but the rest was all gain.

My friend Richard Beach suffered plenty in his life, but he always dealt with it by saying, "Affliction colors your life, but you get to choose the color!"

We chose Refinement Gold.

I don't particularly like who I was before 1991. But I very much like who I've become since my release on September 14, 1992.

Am I the best person you've ever met? No way! Quiet, calm, patient? Not hardly, but much improved.

Perfect? Not this side of heaven. Just emptied of myself and full of God's Spirit much more frequently than before.

And prepared to serve Christ every day with a heart and spirit that can answer the question, "How are you today, Bo?"

I set the paper down. How am I?

Never better, thanks.

And you?

The Keys to Freedom

Are you feeling like you're on the bench? On the shelf? On the receiving end of hard times? Are you like I was, imprisoned by the need to prove your worth? Chained by illness or depression like Gari was? You are not alone.

As we've shared our story over the years to encourage others, we've discovered something interesting.

Usually people listen with interest when Gari and I share how grateful we are that our experiences helped us grow in a positive way. Sometimes they even applaud when we share our joy in knowing Christ. But most interesting to us is that over half the people begin to cry when we ask if they might be in some type of "prison."

And we ask that same question of you. What prison might you be facing that has you feeling trapped, discouraged, upset, broken, or disillusioned about life?

It's almost certain that at some point in your life you will get a phone call, an e-mail, or a diagnosis from a doctor that examines the sturdiness of your life's foundation. You will be forced to ask yourself, "Have I unintentionally built my entire life on sand that's going to sink, and in the process, destroy me? Or have I built my life on the solid foundation, the bedrock of Jesus Christ?" Scripture tells us that He is the only solid foundation you can build on (Matthew 7:24-27).

As we journeyed through our nightmare and into the arms of God, He clearly revealed several key truths that lead to the freedom only Jesus can give. I'd like to share three that may help you, too. But before I do, consider asking yourself these questions:

"What trap do I feel I can never escape?"

"What difficulty seems too hard to overcome?"

"What causes me to cry?"

Will you share your answers with God? Can you make your trial or difficulty a God deal? No matter what your prison is, you can use these keys to find freedom—beginning today.

1. *God loves you and wants a relationship with you.*

> Here I am! I [Jesus Christ] stand at the door and knock. If anyone hears my voice and opens the door, I will come in and eat with him, and he with me.
>
> REVELATION 3:20

Jesus Christ not only wants a relationship with you, but He also wants to free you from your prison. Begin by opening the door to Him, confessing your sins, and asking for His forgiveness.

> Come, let's talk this over, says the Lord; no matter how deep the stain of your sins, I can take it out and make you as clean as freshly fallen snow. Even if you are stained as red as crimson, I can make you white as wool!
>
> ISAIAH 1:18, TLB

Jesus doesn't simply forgive you and unlock your prison doors; He says that if you believe He is the Son of God, He will "give you the keys of the kingdom of heaven" (Matthew 16:19). Imagine that: You can enter a kingdom whose ruler loves you so much that He sent His Son to die on a Cross so you could have eternal life. All you need to do is believe in Him (John 3:16).

If you believe in Jesus, you can begin a new life (2 Corinthians 5:17)! With God's help, you'll be able to deal with any trouble life may bring your way.

I've learned that forgiveness plays a role in our relationship with God. Because He has forgiven us, He wants us to forgive anyone who has hurt us even though it's not always easy (Matthew 18:21-22).

Most offenses are small and easy to forgive. I usually tell myself, "Play it down, pray it up, and blow it off" when a small offense occurs. Give it to God, take it as a part of life, and don't make an issue of it.

But when someone goes out of his or her way to cause pain by telling partial truths that damage reputations or break hearts, or even cause physical harm, that may call for an even greater effort to forgive.

I needed to make that effort to forgive the banker who wasn't 100 percent honest and the person who chose to lie about me while I was in prison. Some of those lies remain in people's minds to this day, so every time the issue comes up, I need to forgive those men again. Forgiveness keeps me free from the prison of grudges that would otherwise exist.

As Gari says: "If we don't forgive, we risk damaging our souls and destroying our lives with bitterness and anger. If we don't forgive, we jeopardize the freedom that comes from Christ. God commands forgiveness because we receive His very best when we forgive."

Asking God to help us forgive others and be reconciled with them if possible seems to be His path to healthy and free living. I know it worked that way for our family through our crisis.

As you pray about these things, you can be sure that God hears your prayers. Prayer is our means of communication with God, so pray as much as you can. Talking to and listening to God leads to freedom! In fact, the Bible says that the prayer of a person who is right with God is powerful and effective (James 5:16) and presenting your requests to God with thanksgiving brings peace (Philippians 4:6-7).

On your darkest day, remember one more thing: God performs miracles! He can change your situation, your perspective—anything—in an instant. If your situation requires a miracle as amazing as the Red Sea parting, then pray for that! Ask God to move as only He can. But as you ask, keep in mind that God's timing and your timing won't always be the same. His timing is perfect, and only He knows what's best for you.

2. *God is in control, and because He is, you can find hope and fresh meaning in life.*

> And we know that in all things God works for the
> good of those who love him, who have been called
> according to his purpose. For those God foreknew
> he also predestined to be conformed to the likeness
> of his Son, that he might be the firstborn among
> many brothers. And those he predestined, he also
> called; those he called, he also justified; those he
> justified, he also glorified.
>
> ROMANS 8:28-30

After Ted Blank and I entered into a contract to purchase Mercy Hospital—but before we completed the transaction—a hospital group in Nevada offered us a generous sum of money to purchase our position. We could have stopped our work immediately and felt good that we had been blessed in a big way.

But Gari had other thoughts.

"God is in control of this transaction," she said. "And obviously you and Ted have done a wise thing or this group wouldn't have made the offer. I think God has a bigger blessing planned. Why don't you complete the purchase and wait on the Lord to see what happens?"

We closed on the original deal, owned the hospital for 13 months, and then sold it to a happy group of doctors for 10 times the profit we would have made on the Nevada offer. Wow! I had almost anchored my happiness to a small blessing compared to what God had in mind!

That real estate deal is my reminder that God is in control and I'm not. I had pushed Him out of the driver's seat of my life and taken the wheel back into my own hands. But God is the best driver because He wants the absolute best for us and is ready to give us hope and a new beginning.

Have you turned loose of the wheel? Let God do the driving in your life! This will give you peace when you realize that He knows your problems and wants to help you if you'll allow Him to.

Even when it seems all is lost, God is still in control and you can hope in Him. If you've sinned and that has led to your prison, God wants to forgive you. Just ask for and receive that forgiveness, knowing He wants you to start over with a clean slate!

No matter what placed you behind your own bars, believe Romans 8:28—that God can bring good out of your situation.

And consider these verses:

I remember my affliction and my wandering,
    the bitterness and the gall.
I well remember them,
    and my soul is downcast within me.
Yet this I call to mind
    and therefore I have hope:

Because of the LORD's great love we are not consumed,
    for his compassions never fail.
They are new every morning;
    great is your faithfulness.
I say to myself, "The LORD is my portion;
    therefore I will wait for him."

LAMENTATIONS 3:19-24

So as you hope in the Lord, hold on to this truth: The Creator of life knows you and has a great future for you (Jeremiah 29:11)! Ephesians 2:8-10 says you are God's handiwork, created in Christ Jesus to do good works, which God prepared in advance for you to do.

While I was behind bars, God showed me He loves me just the way I am, but He loves me so much that He wants me to grow into all I can be in Christ. He has that same message for you! Philippians 1:6 tells us to be "confident of this, that he who began a good work in you will carry it on to completion until the day of Christ Jesus."

To begin stepping into the future God has for you, make a list of everything positive in your life and ask God for the hope He wants you to have.

3. *Seek to live every day to please Him, drawing wisdom and strength from His Word and the wise counselors He puts in your life.*

> For you were once darkness, but now you are light in the Lord. Live as children of light (for the fruit of the light consists in all goodness, righteousness and truth) and find out what pleases the Lord.
>
> EPHESIANS 5:8-10

I was falling back into the trap of being a people-pleaser rather than a God-pleaser during my 10 years of work with the Teammates for Kids Foundation.

Each year our foundation attracted hundreds of donors, and each year we had hundreds of worthy charities asking us for money. A lot of strings were tied to me once again. I could feel myself being pulled back into the habit of moving too fast and trying to do too much.

But before I made things worse for myself and those involved in the foundation, God provided me with a respectful "means of escape." I'll always view my experience with

Teammates for Kids as a God deal and a good deal, but in 2007, it was time for me to move on.

I quickly moved back to focusing more on God's Word and paying more attention to wise counsel from people who love me and love the Lord. My personal protection team was in full agreement when I left the foundation.

Teammates for Kids continued to succeed without my help, and I avoided the pain I'd caused years before when my pride and ego got out of control.

So let me ask you: What's the North Star on the compass of your life? Is it people? Is it projects? Is it money? Is it anything other than God? A life lived to please Christ leads to the most joyful and successful existence possible!

Reading the Bible—God's Word—will help you to know what pleases God. Learn what He expects of you, so you can "stay always within the boundaries where God's love can reach and bless you" (Jude 1:21, TLB). I've discovered that it's easier to make right choices daily, because many wrong choices in the little things of life often lead to wrong choices in the major decisions.

What you believe and do should align with what the Bible says, not with what you see on the Internet and TV, read in other books, or hear from well-meaning friends who may offer advice not based on God's Word. Read the Bible daily to maintain your focus on Jesus and gain strength and wisdom.

The Bible also tells us to choose partners and friends wisely (Proverbs 12:26). God wants us to encourage each other (1 Thessalonians 5:11), and He is able to put fellow believers in your life who can do that and give you wise counsel. The Bible says that the way of fools seems right to them, but the wise listen to advice (Proverbs 12:15).

You can do what I did: Ask God to help you assemble your personal protection team. It should consist of wise people who love Christ, want the best for you, and will have the courage to say "No," if that's what you need to hear.

So don't waste another minute behind the bars of your prison! Take hold of Jesus Christ's keys to freedom today. With Christ's love and grace in your life, your best days are ahead of you. And someday soon, when people ask how you are, you'll be able to say, "Never better."

Acknowledgments

We are forever grateful to the following family members and friends whose love for Christ and care for our family lifted us above the circumstances of our darkest days and continued to give us hope during our recovery years. You always made us feel accepted and celebrated.

To all the people who prayed for Gari and helped in so many ways during her illness, with special thanks to Helen and Everett Dye. We also are grateful to Don and Diane Reeverts and their daughter, Ashley, as well as Gehl and Marsha Caldwell and their son Chad, who supported our children through friendship, meals, and comfort during this time.

To Bo's roommates in prison who helped to make his life bearable.

To Philip and Nancy Anschutz and Sue Anschutz-Rodgers for treating us with a kindness rarely seen in the business world.

To the Denver Nuggets players and staff members, for standing with Bo when it would have been easier to replace him as team chaplain.

To Jim Dobson for defending us so lovingly and walking by our side every step of the way. Being guests on his radio show helped us begin rebuilding our lives, and his appointment of Bo as emcee of the Focus on the Family Couples Retreats gave us a safe place to continue our healing process.

To the Doulos Ministry staff and board members, especially our lifelong friends Richard and Marsha Beach, for giving Bo a chance to rebuild our financial lives, and for celebrating our contribution to their ministry.

To the Furniture Row team, especially Barney and Carolyn Visser, for believing in us and giving us the gift of being a small part of their amazing company.

To Shirley Dobson for giving us the opportunity to create the Colorado Council for the National Day of Prayer, and to all of our incredible council friends who have served with us as we pray for our nation.

To MOPS International for giving Gari opportunities to serve as a mentor, board member, and consultant.

To the staff and board members of the Teammates for Kids Foundation, especially Howard Parker and Greg Anderson, for a decade of partnership in helping kids around the world, and for the wonderful memories we made along the way.

To the past and present board members of Crosswalk Fellowship and the fantastic CWF staff, especially president Susie Hayes, for positive energy, encouragement, and creativity in the launch and building of a meaningful ministry.

To the men of Narrow Gate, a ministry of CWF, with a special thank you to Mark Klibbe for the encouragement he gives us each week and his faithfulness to Christ.

To Dr. Bob Beltz and his wife, Allison, for more than 35 years of great ministry partnership.

To the Game Day Memories staff and board members, especially Paul Andrews, for allowing us the joy of seeing deserving kids and their families experience happiness, laughter, and love.

To our friends at the Colorado Rockies, especially Dick Monfort and Jackie and Dan O'Dowd, for involving Bo as a consultant and including both of us in our roles as team chaplain and Bible teacher.

To everyone who endorsed our book: Each one of you encouraged us in different ways, and we are grateful for the time, thought, and care that went into writing each endorsement.

To the Focus on the Family staff and board of directors, especially Ken Windebank, who had the original idea that our story would help others and be a great fit as a Focus project. We want to especially thank Julie Holmquist, our main editor, for her helpful insight and advice. And to Bob DeMoss, Larry Weeden, and our cowriter, John Duckworth, we are eternally grateful. Thanks also to all the wonderful people at Focus in the marketing, editing, legal, design, and theology departments, and the team of professionals at Tyndale House Publishers, Inc., for their excellent work in helping our story come to life.

To Jerry Jenkins for being a friend and investing his time and talent to write our book's foreword, and for his insightful edits. Thanks a million times over!

To Joe and Gail Coors for their friendship in all things, with very special thanks for believing our story would encourage others.

Finally, to our dear family members for your prayers, financial support, and thoughtful concern for us expressed in phone calls, letters, visits, and numerous other ways. You are the best. Thanks for sharing life with us!

And eternally, we thank our Lord and Savior, Jesus Christ.

Notes

1. From "What a Wonderful World" by Bob Thiele and George David Weiss, © 1967 Carlin America Inc., BMG Rights Management U.S., LLC, Imagem U.S., LLC.
2. Oswald Chambers, *My Utmost for His Highest* (Grand Rapids, MI: Discovery House Publishers, 1989), 312.
3. "Colorado's Mount Lindo Cross," *Cemeteries and Cemetery Symbols*, https://cemeteries.wordpress.com/2007/03/16/colorados-mount-lindo-cross/.
4. Michael Wells, *Sidetracked in the Wilderness* (Littleton, CO: Abiding Life Press, 1991, 1999), 48.
5. Ibid., 76.
6. Ibid., 77.
7. Ibid., 85–86.
8. Ibid., 86.
9. Ibid., 123, italics in the original.
10. Gary Smalley with Al Janssen, *Joy That Lasts* (Grand Rapids, MI: Zondervan, 1986, 1988), 9.
11. Ibid., 49.

12. Ibid., 50.
13. Ibid.
14. Ibid., 57.
15. From "Learning to Live Again" by Donald Alan Schlitz Jr. and Stephanie Davis, © 1993 Universal Music/MGB Songs.
16. Felisa Cardona, "Nottingham Resigns Amid Probe," *Denver Post*, Wednesday, October 21, 2008, 1.
17. From "My Dad" by Barry Mann and Cynthia Weil, © 1962 Sony/ATV Music Publishing, LLC.

ONE LIFE SHATTERED, ONE MAN SAVED

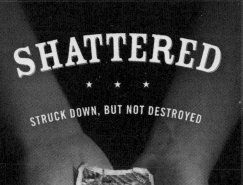

FRANK PASTORE
WITH ELLEN VAUGHN

Cincinnati Reds pitcher Frank Pastore's Major League Baseball career was shattered when his elbow was smashed by a direct hit. *Shattered* is the story of how God uses broken dreams for greater purposes.

★ ★ ★

AVAILABLE WHEREVER CHRISTIAN BOOKS ARE SOLD. CP1109

Meet the rest of the family

Expert advice on parenting and marriage . . . spiritual growth . . . powerful personal stories . . .

Focus on the Family's collection of inspiring, practical resources can help your family grow closer to God—and each other—than ever before. Whichever format you need—video, audio, book, or e-book—we have something for you. Discover how to help your family thrive with books, DVDs, and more at **FocusOnTheFamily.com/resources**.

FOCUS ON THE FAMILY®

Welcome to the Family ———

Whether you purchased this book, borrowed it, or received it as a gift, thanks for reading it! This is just one of many insightful, biblically based resources that Focus on the Family produces for people in all stages of life.

Focus is a global Christian ministry dedicated to helping families thrive as they celebrate and cultivate God's design for marriage and experience the adventure of parenthood. Our outreach exists to support individuals and families in the joys and challenges they face, and to equip and empower them to be the best they can be.

Through our many media outlets, we offer help and hope, promote moral values and share the life-changing message of Jesus Christ with people around the world.

Focus on the Family MAGAZINES

These faith-building, character-developing publications address the interests, issues, concerns, and challenges faced by every member of your family from preschool through the senior years.

For More INFORMATION

ONLINE:
Log on to
FocusOnTheFamily.com
In Canada, log on to
FocusOnTheFamily.ca

PHONE:
Call toll-free:
**800-A-FAMILY
(232-6459)**
In Canada, call toll-free:
800-661-9800

THRIVING FAMILY® Marriage & Parenting	FOCUS ON THE FAMILY CLUBHOUSE JR.® Ages 4 to 8	FOCUS ON THE FAMILY CLUBHOUSE® Ages 8 to 12	FOCUS ON THE FAMILY CITIZEN® U.S. news issues

Rev. 3/11
CP0552